Unlock the Power to Feed Your Soul

A Recipe for Transformative Self-Care

by Alison M English

for mom

You were fostering my creativity long before I recognized it.
Thanks for always pointing me back to this
fundamental piece that lived deep within my soul.

.

Table of Contents

4

What Gets In the Way

5

Application

A few words before we start...

I kind of like to know what I'm getting into before I start something, so I think it is important that you understand a few things about me, who this book is intended for and generally what to expect.

I am not a therapist, a theologian or a scientist. I am a regular person, with a job, a family and the general limitations that we often call "first world problems." I am a normal person living a life that looks very similar to the lives of many women around me with normal issues, challenging schedules, kids, a career and a marriage to boot.

The sentiments I share in this book are based on my own personal discovery, data I have gleaned from other women around me, and interviews with a variety of people who have discovered something similar in their own lives.

Since this book was written from my perspective as a woman and because my surveys and interviews were conducted with women, I decided to speak directly to women. But I do believe that the principles shared apply to both sexes and people of any age. While I claim Christianity as my faith, and I will speak about it, this book is for anyone in any walk of faith (or not). If you believe in beauty, the need for balance and the need to nourish your soul in such a way that brings you greater contentment, gratitude, and peace, then this book is for you.

What you get out of this book is really up to you. I don't know where you are coming from, where you are intending to go, or what challenges you are facing. I don't know your age, if you are a wife or a mom, or if you have religious beliefs. But I do know this: you are here because most likely, in some way, you are tired. You are stressed. You may be anxious and struggling to handle it all. You feel like life should have more meaning and purpose. You feel you should be more content, appreciative and grateful for this life you have been given.

I also have yet to meet a woman who didn't in some way feel like she wasn't enough, regardless of her age, race or spirituality. For some reason, there seems to be a belief inside of all of us that something is wrong or broken or not worthy. If any of these things describes you today, let me tell you something: you are worthy of giving something to yourself that brings forth life, joy, and complete awe. You are worthy of beauty and hope and gratitude. You are worthy of giving yourself a moment to relish in something that is super meaningful to you. And you are worthy of the love and adoration you will find in discovering how to feed your soul.

My ask, when those feelings of unworthiness start to come up, is to remind yourself that I began by telling you that you are, indeed, worthy of nourishing your soul. You may just be surprised how desperately you need it. Though your personal journey will be unique, my goal is to help you recognize this need and show you ways to help fulfill it.

Introduction

"One life on this earth is all we get, whether it is enough or not enough, and the obvious conclusion would seem to be that at the very least we are fools if we do not live it as fully and bravely and beautifully as we can."

Fredrick Buechner

My Story

Ah, to live fully and bravely and beautifully. I think this is what the little girl of my childhood dreamt of when she thought of growing up. But when adulthood showed up and all the realities and responsibilities hit, living fully, bravely, and beautifully almost felt impossible. If I'm honest, at times, it felt like a fairytale I was sold that became a lie.

I remember asking myself through a lot of my adult life – isn't life supposed to feel more beautiful than this? There were beautiful moments, but something just seemed lacking. And I resigned myself to the fact that like many of my childhood fantasies, maybe I was expecting just a little too much from what life had to offer.

But I had an awakening, an "aha," a revelation from God that maybe I was looking at this whole thing the wrong way. Maybe I was missing it. Maybe life was supposed to feel fuller and more beautiful. And I discovered it in the act of nourishing my soul.

As a Christian, I grew up believing that "soul care" was predominantly done through religious acts and rituals. It was done through prayer, memorization, and attending church on the regular. These were all pieces of my daily life and I was still asking this fundamental question. Isn't life supposed to be more beautiful?

So, if this foundational belief was coming up short, then what did it mean to feed my soul? I practiced self-care after all. Was that it? And as I pondered this topic, I was immediately struck with a correlation to food - actual food - and how it serves many purposes in our ability to live well.

I grew up in the deep South. A small town in South Alabama. The South is known for it's comfort food and as a native my world was heavily influenced by the food served in restaurants, around the picnic table, from friends and neighbors. My idea of good food came deeply rooted from this place. My culture in the South is heavily influenced by African American culture and soul food is a large part of that heritage. Southern food and soul food in the deep South were nearly synonymous - difficult to see where one started and the other ended.

When I think of the term "soul food," nostalgia rushes in. Fried chicken, cornbread, biscuits and honey, butter slathered on just about everything and greens cooked to perfection. There is a reason why soul food is considered comfort food because in every sense of the word it is just that. Think about how it makes you feel—warm, full, satiated, verifiably content and maybe just a little guilty.

But if you dig deeper into the origins of soul food, you will discover there is a difference. These hearty recipes were born out of necessity and survival. Soul food evolved from African American influences during slavery. It's very inception came from a place of need, to have a delicious and caloric meal to refuel after a hard, tumultuous, and painful day's work. Meals were prepared from rations given by slave owners - food low in quality and little nutritional value. Preserving their African food traditions, slaves used what they had to make the food satisfying. These traditions birthed a style of cooking that is enjoyed far beyond its roots in the deep South today. And out of a horrific time in our country's history, this comforting and sustaining food was born.

It was an analogy that struck me. Today, when we experience pain and suffering in our very comfortable lives, soul food looks very different. The soul food that I am referring to, as you will learn, is not born out of our pain, but it is there to sustain us through the hardships. It is there to foster much-needed gratitude. It is there to point us heavenward. It is there to allow us to see all the beauty, richness and blessings that are bestowed on us every day. It serves a meaningful purpose, and I was missing it. It was through my personal pain and suffering that I realized my utter need for it.

On the morning of my forty-first birthday I awoke feeling exhausted, angry, forlorn, and trapped. I was almost finished with one of the largest and most stressful projects in my career. There were looming deadlines at work. I had just moved my family from the burbs to the city in the middle of the school year, downsizing from a 5,000 square foot home to 1,300. I had taken over the reins as my husband stepped out of his 15-year career to figure out what was next. I started my kids in new schools, and had my heart broken over a role I desperately wanted at work. To say I felt depleted and worn out is an absolute understatement.

I wanted out badly. I was hurt, broken, lonely, and so tired. The trapped feeling of being controlled by my circumstances left me mentally and emotionally clawing at the surface. I was screaming to get out, but I had no choice but to push through it all. I felt stuck.

I remember my mother saying, "I don't know how you are handling all of this stress at once. It is a lot. I'm surprised you haven't come undone." But what are you going to do when everything feels like it is completely out of your control? Losing it wasn't going to help anything, and I didn't feel like I had a choice.

Finding the grit to push through is not an unfamiliar territory for me. I had to do it throughout my fundamentalist Christian upbringing, when my husband was in grad school and I was laid off with two kids, and when my marriage was falling apart. I know how to dig deep and muster through.

But when I woke up on September 24, 2019, I realized something. I had pushed through and made it to the "other side." I had accomplished my goals, was meeting my deadlines, and had moved my family, but for what? I was consumed by my circumstances and completely lost myself in the process. I thought, how in the world do I keep this from happening again?

And that is when God hit me with it. He had given me the answer long ago—I just didn't understand it. I had failed to use it.

The secret was in the metaphorical principle of "soul food." It was in nourishing my soul. You see, my circumstances may have been out of my control, but the reason I felt trapped by them is that I had allowed them to control me. I dug deep and mustered through the pain and suffering that were results of my current circumstances, but I was starving.

My soul was starving for something to sustain and nourish it. While I couldn't control what was going on around me, I could control how I took care of myself. This principle of feeding my soul represented just the nourishment I needed to combat the stress and anxiety of my circumstances. But I had failed to eat. I told myself I didn't have time. I couldn't create the space. There wasn't a place for me to nourish myself. And we all know that starvation will kill you.

section 1

Building the
Foundation

I

What Is Feeding Your Soul?

Knowing what fueled me came in time, but I didn't recognize it when it first showed up. I would have moments that would spark a fire in my belly. I would feel it, know it, and in that brief glimpse into the magic, I would be overcome--overcome with emotion and gratitude. It was like a jewel, a gift, a brief pause hanging in the space of time.

To describe it is almost impossible, but when you experience it, you know. It's almost as if time doesn't exist. You feel such an overwhelming sense of happiness and joy. The feelings almost overcome you to the point where you feel like you want to weep or laugh out loud. It is almost as if your body can't help but respond to it. It can take your breath away.

And then the moment would be gone in a flash. I'd never know when it would hit again. It always seemed to find me in the quiet, when I was alone or literally staring at my children sleeping. It would show up watching the light glistening over the water at the beach or the sun peering through the trees, and there it was—strong, deep and overwhelming. Contentment would wash over me again: it was spiritual.

It's funny; I never connected these experiences to my creativity, but now looking back, I see the connection. A talented music teacher once told me to feel the music as I played. I was puzzled. How do you do that? And then one day, I mastered a song and playing it felt like an out-of-body experience. I finally understood what it was to feel the music, and it was magic.

This piece of me seemed to lay dormant after I was grown and married. There were sparks, but I never knew how to keep them. I would yearn for them, but they would only appear when I was least expecting them. Again, this magic would appear when I was quiet and alone.

A couple of years ago, I had this yearning curiosity. There were things that I wanted to try. I wanted to paint. I decided I wouldn't let the year pass without giving it a go. I had never approached a canvas without a plan, and I wanted to see what it was like. It took me nearly six months to schedule my "session" (which was literally me driving to my closest art supply store and grabbing a few items). I lit a candle, turned on some soft tunes, and approached the canvas. And there it was, this magic, this flow, this beautiful and overwhelming feeling of joy and peace. I walked away from the experience in awe and with deep gratitude.

I thought, there is no way this magic can appear again. It was a fluke, right? I went to the canvas again and again only to find that the magic always found me there. And I started noticing other things that were fueling me if I'd only notice—photography, writing, walking through a meadow, riding bikes with my kids, arranging flowers, sketching, lighting a candle, drinking my morning cup of coffee, and the list goes on.

The magic was happening all around me. It was like the exercise of creating unlocked something in my soul, and gratitude poured out. It got me thinking: is this one of the secrets to living a meaningful life? Is it the practice of the things that are innately woven into our beings? The things that are so much a part of our wiring that if we suppress them, ignore them, or never discover them, we will fail to find satisfaction? Is it the practice of these things that makes the magic more acute? I found that as I was more in tune with caring for my soul through creativity, my awareness was heightened.

I found my spiritual life was sparked as well. It was the closest to God I had ever felt. I was experiencing something almost akin to worship. Were these gifts of love from above? Was this what it could mean to feel like you were in a real relationship with God? It was something that felt special, personal, and I yearned for more.

I've wrestled with these conclusions since their onset. What did they mean, and why did it take me so long to discover a very simple principle? The reason, I have come to realize, is that I believe many of us are starving. We are busy, overwhelmed and carrying the burdens and hurts of others. We are caring for our children, our families, and our spouses. We have careers and families. We are exhausted and tired. We are doers, pursuers, and many of us aren't even paying attention to how we are feeling. We are anxious and find that our faith, prayer, and Scripture reading come up null. Our busyness is in overdrive, and our lives are full of distractions.

I didn't have a clue how I was feeling because I learned to live in the chaos. I then would look to escape by checking out in a myriad of ways, but this didn't help. I began to feel like I was going to scream.

And then guilt would set in…

Wasn't this life everything I wanted? Everything I had dreamed of? Then why did I feel so unhappy? Why did I rush to get my kids into bed? Why was I so frustrated at work? Why was I so discontent in my relationships? Why was finding gratitude so hard?

I now know it's because I was failing to feed my soul—that was the missing piece. All those feelings were symptoms. They were symptoms of a soul so depleted of nourishment that I couldn't find the peace and gratitude necessary to show up well, love my life, and relish in the magical everyday moments.

And that, my friends, is the purpose of feeding your soul.

2

Soul *vs* Ego

Before we can get into how to find and practice feeding your soul, I think it is important to talk about a few fundamentals. Without this foundation, it can be hard to uncover what may be going on deep down, and I personally have found that definitions and awareness help.

Our person, I believe, is made up of both soul and ego. They are not the same, but they exist together. I mention both of them because they are both necessary, but I'm not sure we think about these two things together. Our egos are useful things. They can help us stand up for ourselves. They can help us achieve our goals and dreams. And like many things, egos can have an evil side as well—one that is detrimental. My ego was one of the things that was heavily contributing to my misery on my forty-first birthday.

I mention it because in the vast wealth of American society (and quite possibly the first world), our egos are heavily cultivated in our upbringing so that we can bring forth the successes and gains in the opportunistic worlds we live in. This is important because some-

times it may be hard to discover your soul because the ego is cultivated and strong while the soul, in some cases, is lying dormant, or
even mute.

This means that much of the time, we live out of our egos and not
our souls. We will compromise the yearnings of our souls to appease
the ego. We may even mistake soul yearnings when they are really
desires coming from the ego. This means many times the yearnings
of our soul aren't even a part of the equation. Our egos are driving
so much that the soul is lying dormant, even neglected.

How do I know this? Well, just ask yourself, when was the last time
you got offended or frustrated by something? Yes, there are times
where your boundaries are violated or someone takes advantage or
is mean or ugly, but many times your reaction is because your ego
gets bruised.

This happened to me recently. I was asked to do something at
work. At the start, a leader had requested that I help his team with
something. I was flattered, so much so that I told a few friends and
family members. It felt good to be sought after. Then I found out
what the work was, and I was offended. The work felt beneath my
skill level. I began worrying about my perception. Why wasn't I seen
differently? Maybe they didn't think I was smart enough for another "more important" job. Why couldn't they see that I was capable
of more—you know like that big, sexy, vital-to-the-business project?
Why wasn't I getting called for that?

Then I thought about this whole concept. Had I taken one second to get quiet, stop, and listen to my soul? No. I was so driven by
my ego that I had let insecurity set in, causing embarrassment and
even anger. Instead, guess what happened when I quieted my ego?
I may not find the work all that interesting, but at my core, my de-

sire is to help, add value, and serve a purpose. It's not about being better than certain tasks or being given "sexy work." But my ego was in overdrive. I failed to see and appreciate what this meaningful ask meant. I failed to find gratitude in being seen as someone they could trust to get the job done.

Which brings us to this: what is a soul? It can be defined in many ways, but I love this interpretation from *dictionary.com*:

"The soul is defined as the principle of life, feeling, thought, and action in humans, regarded as a distinct entity separate from the body, and commonly held to be separable in existence from the body; the spiritual part of humans as distinct from the physical part. The spiritual part of humans regarded in its moral aspect, or as believed to survive death and be subject to happiness or misery in a life to come."

The soul is the spiritual part of our being—the piece many of us believe will live on after our bodies are gone. If you think about it, it is the source of your heart—not your physical heart, but your human one--the heart that loves, cares for, and yearns. It is where your passion comes from, your personality, your moral compass, and the reservoir of your feelings and emotions. It is where you come alive and where you can feel injured and alone. Your soul is you.

But the ego is there inside of you too. I picture them sitting side by side like two friends that either exist together in a healthy way until one overbearingly tries to rule the other. They are buried deep down inside of my person, and many of my actions and feelings are born out of that space.

I'd never really thought about how these two things exist, impact one another, and live together until I started this work. I believe there is value in learning to cultivate the soul in such a way that it brings these two pieces of ourselves into a healthier balance. We have to recognize how our egos may be getting in the way or clouding the very thing that our souls actually need, and in doing this we can live a more meaningful and joyful life. I also believe recognizing these two distinct pieces of ourselves can help one come closer to discovering what is actually fueling his or her soul, which is why I bring it up.

To add a little clarity, I like the way Richard Rohr explains these two paradigms in his book *Everything Belongs*. He says, "the soul doesn't know itself by comparison and differentiation [like our egos]. The soul just is. The soul knows itself through what is now and everything that is both the dark and the light. The soul triumphs over nothing and therefore cannot be defeated because it is not in the game of succeeding or failing. It does not need to separate the dark from the light. Everything belongs" (pg. 72).

The ego on the other hand, "It is the dualist inside of us." He references James Carse stating "It is the habit of seeing ourselves over and against someone else." Richard goes on to say, "That is exactly what the ego wants to do—to my ego my wealth, my intelligence, my moral goodness, and my social class are what they are only in contrast to the person next to me. But the still center, my true self, does not need to oppose, differentiate, or compare itself" (pg. 72). He goes on to say that our soul is okay and even satisfied with the "enoughness" of the present moment. And it is here that we are in touch with reality.

When explained this way, it helps me realize how much of my life is being driven out of ego instead of the still, quiet places of my soul. There is this constant level of comparison—this place of always seeking to be over and above. You could call that drive, and I'm not saying it is a bad thing, but when it clouds my ability to hear the yearning of my soul and to understand how to nourish it, it becomes a problem. This is why it's easy for me to see why my life, stress, and so many other things get off kilter. My ego is in overdrive and my soul… well, I'm not sure. I think it is ignored.

Take for instance the example I gave above. If I learned to stop when I start feeling my feathers ruffle over a project I didn't like and ask myself, "Are these feelings coming from my ego or from my soul?" The way I might respond might be different. I'm pretty sure I'd lean more into finding gratitude that someone saw me as a helper *vs* questioning my perception.

Let me give you another example. When I started painting, I didn't recognize exactly what it was giving me. It wasn't until this revelation that I determined why I was painting. But before I landed here, my ego started driving, and I began to resent the thing that brought me joy.

In my heart of hearts, I am an entrepreneur. It is very difficult for me to start something and not ask myself how I can make money at it. When I started painting, six months later I had set up shop and was selling my work online. The only problem: no one was buying. And my ego got really bruised.

Why? Because I saw the purchase of my work as validation. I saw it as an affirmation of my talent and worth. It was that "over and above" thing—a desire to be "better than." I realized that sharing my work wasn't about sharing something that brought me joy. It also wasn't about the money. It was about my ego having the affirmation or the permission to keep doing it.

If I had painted merely out of the depths of my soul, none of this would have mattered. I didn't need to sell my work in order to have permission or validation to keep painting. Selling doesn't increase my value as a human being or make me "better than." Painting out of my ego certainly didn't feed my soul. When I focused my worth on the number of sales I was getting from my paintings, the joy disappeared.

I share this paradigm more for awareness. I believe the "how" of leading from your soul *vs* your ego takes a good bit of work, and honestly, feeding my soul has become a big part of that. I state the difference between the two because, much like this discovery of needing soul care, I also didn't realize just how much my ego was showing up and getting in the way.

In a foundational sense, nourishing and cultivating the soul quiets the ego and puts it in its proper place, resulting in joy and gratitude with the present. If you let yourself really think about this shift in paradigm, it powerfully sets the stage for the journey we are about to embark on.

3

What a Depleted Soul Looks Like

My hope with the descriptions of both soul and ego, while complex, is to help ground you as you search to nourish your soul. It will also raise your awareness on how your ego could play a role in this discovery. You could probably perform many activities out of your ego (and I'd argue that many of us have experiences like my painting). I say this not to blame, but so you recognize it.

I also can tell you that I originally didn't know I needed to feed my soul. I didn't have any awareness of just how much I was living out of my ego. But I discovered through my suffering that I had a misbalanced sense of what taking good care of myself should look like and how much my ego was involved. My self-care practices had little to do with my soul, and the reality was, I wasn't really taking care of myself. It's one of the reasons I woke up unhappy on my birthday.

And to be honest, this whole self-care thing is quite the buzz word these days. There are a lot of opinions on the topic and many suggestions on what it should and shouldn't look like. I even read an article that encouraged self-care while also making me feel bad about wanting to do the things I really liked. It suggested more exercise, green veggies and told me to get over my bubble baths. What? Why is there judgment in self-care? Self-care has almost become like dieting—it's hard to even know what is "good" these days. The thing is, I believed in it, but I had never really put much thought into what "it" was, and I certainly wasn't viewing it from the position of my soul.

I knew that in order to show up well, I needed to take care of myself, but I rarely prioritized it; and when I did, I was rarely good at it. I generally found that while some of the activities were good, all I was really doing was focusing on checking out. Checking out was easy. It required no thought or planning and could happen even when I didn't necessarily want it to.

I found myself spending endless hours on social media or binging Netflix. I'm not sure I knew there was any other way to refuel, and I got to the point where I didn't want to feel like I was just "checking off" my days. Sadly, checking out wasn't even checking the box anymore. I was still coming up short, feeling overtired and stuck.

I woke up on my birthday thinking, "I'm more miserable than I was a year ago." I was starting to notice that my mood was negatively affecting things around me. Let me describe what complete depletion of soul looks like. When you are not feeding your soul, you will feel an overwhelming sense of frustration. You feel so stuck that you feel like you could scream. You can feel trapped. You are tired and weary. This makes you anxious, angry, ungrateful, and overwhelmed, It takes too much energy to course-correct because you don't know where to start. You go back to checking out because it is easy and the only thing you really know how to do. And the sad thing is, it can become such a part of your cycle that you don't even recognize you are doing it.

If you are like me, this level of frustration sneaks up on you. There are signs present over and over again—almost alarms going off—but you keep ignoring them so that you can take care of all the things that are controlling your life. You can start to feel completely out of control, and when things get this bad, it is usually when you wake up and can't take it anymore.

I had come to such a point that I felt like I was going to crack. Inside I was unhappy. I was looking at everything in my wake and pointing to it like it was the problem (and some of it was), but much of it was because I was stuck in a cyclical pattern that wasn't taking care of me in a way that was feeding my soul. I was starving.

I knew it was bad when I wanted to "take the edge off" with a little too much wine. The numbing had expanded to now needing something to make me feel better. I could tell at the time that this is where substance abuse is born. It happens to the best people with the best intentions, and I knew I was on the edge.

Feeling trapped is something I have felt over and over in my life. I'm not one to be caged, and I'm guessing you aren't either. It's not in our natures. But I'm amazed at how many times I put myself there. I trap myself because I fail to see the patterns and feelings as warning signs—warning signs that I now know mean that I am not really caring for myself. I was simply checking out and not feeding my soul.

I'm guessing I'm not the only one. Just search the web on anxiety, loneliness, and dissatisfaction at work, and you will discover that Americans generally are not very happy. Don't get me wrong, there are a lot of factors that play into this. If you have an anxiety disorder or suffer from depression, please hear me when I say, these aren't just the results of not feeding our souls. These are chronic illnesses just like diabetes, immune disorders, and cancer. But I do believe there are many of us with these symptoms where the culprit is an extreme lack of soul care.

4

Self-Care | Checking Out *vs* Feeding Your Soul
What's the Difference

I don't want to imply that checking out is never good for the soul. I believe that it is necessary. My argument is that checking out is generally our "go to." This is because it is easy and can happen anywhere and anytime. We do it all the time—with television, our phones, and computers. We even check out while we check out, which is where you will sit in front of your television with your computer and phone in your hand scrolling through social media while you are watching a movie.

We also choose to check out in other more destructive ways, and I find that is when my soul is the most depleted. We drink too much, pop a pill, go down a spiraling gossip trail, seek out sex, porn, or you name it. If it will numb us or help "take the edge off," we seek it because we really don't want to feel.

What's funny is we also use busyness to help us check out. Yep, the very thing that we feel is running our lives, we use it. I discovered this for myself during a counseling session where I was shocked at my revelation. I unconsciously was keeping my life in full motion because, and I quote, "I don't want to give myself the space to think or feel." Why? Because I didn't really want to deal with what was going on in my heart and my head. It doesn't help that we also praise and applaud busyness. We wear it like a badge of honor. When you are using busyness to check out, you think you are getting a ton of benefits from it, but are you?

Why don't we feed our souls? We will say it is due to lack of time—and it is. This is a given. There are other reasons too, which we will talk about later. But you want to know the real reason I think most of us don't? We don't know how.

I know this may seem crazy, but every time I go deep with other people on this question they get really stumped. That feeling I described is not even something they experience with their most favorite activities because those activities are still variations of checking out. They are restful practices, which are necessary, and I'm definitely a fan. I've never had a massage where I didn't feel better, but it didn't make me feel magic. It didn't give me that spark. It never gave me an overwhelming sense of gratitude, and it's pretty darn expensive.

Sure, a massage gives me a blissful hour of rest and relaxation, and I would do it regularly if I could afford it; but a massage will never fuel my soul. Unless you have found it—that thing that lights up your soul (and I know it exists in you)—you may have never experienced what I'm talking about. Or like me, it could be such a brief moment and happen so infrequently that I don't even recogize what it was giving me.

Balancing Checking Out and Feeding Your Soul

"The snowflake pattern of your soul is emerging. Each of us is a unique, creative individual. But we often blur that uniqueness with sugar, alcohol, drugs, overwork, underplay, bad relations, toxic sex, under exercise, over-TV, under sleep—many and various forms of junk food for the soul"
The Artist's Way by Julia Cameron (pg 85)

We all know we need to take good care of ourselves, and we all define it differently. Honestly, sometimes it becomes just one more thing on our to-do list that we find a way to feel guilty over (which is crazy) or to not appreciate because we just don't have the time. But just so we are clear in our search for balancing both checking out and feeding the soul, I want to recap a few definitions:

Taking good care (aka self-care)
Doing things or activities to take care of oneself

Checking out
Giving oneself a mental break. It's a desire to avoid thinking deeply or using the body or mind. Activities usually include social media, television, napping, or doing something that doesn't require interaction with other people.

Feeding your soul
Doing an activity that ignites and rejuvenates the soul, bringing feelings of warmth, love, and gratitude.

Also, let me be clear, checking out and feeding your soul are both necessary. I believe that they are both part of self-care. The question is, are you doing both and are they in good balance? In my research with women, I found that you generally know if you are in balance or not. It doesn't take long to ask yourself, am I checking out more than I am feeding my soul? But here is a quick assessment to give you an idea of where you might stand. If you find after doing this activity that you are pretty out of balance and you don't know where to start—like I did—the first step is acknowledging it and then setting out to understand what is, in fact, feeding your soul.

activity

Self-Care *vs* Feeding Your Soul Assessment

Key things to remember:
- One is not better than the other. Both can be good for you.
- Note how each is defined before you get started.
- Review the blank two-by-two grid on page 39 and familiarize yourself with it before you start. Note how the activities you list make you feel and plot them accordingly, i.e. they allow me to check out, but I feel bad, numb, or nothing; or they allow me to check out, and I feel energized.

Directions:

This assessment will allow you to see how much of your self-care activities fall into which category, checking out or feeding the soul. The goal is to determine what activities are serving you well and even determine if you have a balanced approach. Below, list all the activities you enjoy or even use to check out or fuel your soul. Then plot each activity on the chart below to see where these activities fall. See example on next page.

List all activities that you enjoy doing either to check out or to feed your soul using the definitions I have provided.

_____

_____

_____

_____

_____

_____

_____

_____

_____

_____

_____

_____

_____

How to read the grid:

On the next page is a plotting tool. The center represents a neutral zone. At the top of the axis is feeding your soul. At the bottom is checking out. The horizontal line represents how those activities make you feel. They either make you feel bad, numb, or nothing; or they make you feel energized. It is healthiest for you to land above or near the horizontal axis in the healthy quadrants, but you can see for me that things like social media land me in an unhealthy area (see my grid example).

Before you begin plotting, take some time to review my personal examples. It is okay if you aren't sure which activities are which. Just list things you do for yourself and then start plotting them. I have provided you a blank grid at the bottom of this activity or visit my website at www.alisonenglish.com for more info.

My list of go-to activities:
-     Painting
-     Nature walks

- Social media
- Massage
- Taking a bath
- Netflix/watching t.v.
- Lunch with a friend
- Photography
- Cooking

My grid

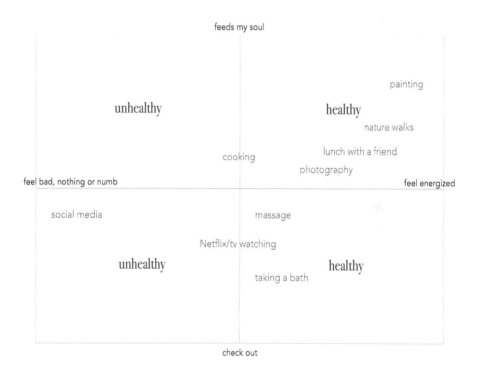

The next step is to go through and put a loose number by each activity. This number represents the number of hours you participate in these activities in a month. See my numbers below in the example I provide (hint: most phones will give you a number on the breakdown of your time on social channels. On an iPhone go to settings/screen time/see all activity. If you click on each app it will give you a daily average breakdown. Take this number and multiply it by number of days in a month to get that app's total. Then add all app totals together to get your final number for social media). Be honest. The point of this exercise is to determine how much you are checking out *vs* feeding your soul, and it can help you determine where you need to create more balance.

My results:

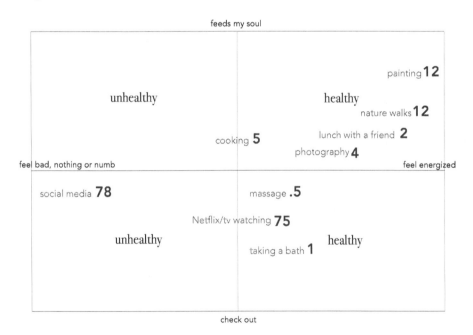

Checking out: 154.5 hours

Feeding my soul: 35 hours

I have quite a gap between these two numbers for the month. For me, this means I need to cut back some on checking out and increase soul care. Defining what this should be is really up to you. I'm not going for an even split, but I'd like to shave off about 30 hours from checking out and add maybe that much onto feeding my soul.

Blank Grid:

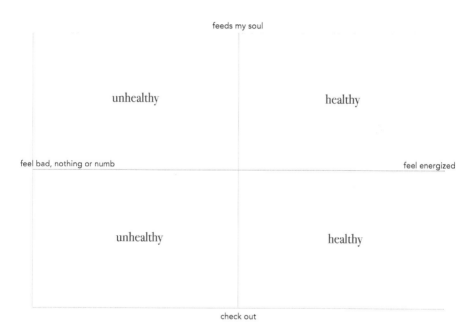

Here is a blank grid for your use, but for the full worksheet please visit my website at www.alisonenglish.com/resources.

section 2

Discovery

5

Discovering What Feeds Your Soul

I believe that what fuels each and every one of us is as unique as our DNA. It is so deep and engrained into our wiring that we literally can't deny it. It's one of the reasons why I have been scared to even approach this subject. It's deeply personal. Even discovering it won't look the same for everyone. But when fear wanted to stop me, I realized that half of the battle is acknowledging that we may not even know what nourishes our souls.

This is my humble attempt to help you find it. There are no guarantees here, just stories, suggestions, and possible tasks to help you get there. You may wonder, if something is so engrained, why don't we always know what it is? If I had to guess, this reason is likely different for every person, but I have some pretty good theories. I will uncover those here and then give you some practical tips for your own journey.

But before we get started, I need you to make a few promises to yourself.

Promise that...

You approach this journey with openness. Don't hold judgement for the process, and listen with both your heart and your mind. Some of you will discover things in an instant, and others may find your journey will form over time—all variations are absolutely okay.

Promise that...

You will fight against your fear. You may unearth things that unnerve you, make you feel vulnerable or even uncomfortable, but I promise these feelings are necessary. They aren't reasons to quit.

You need to know this because you will be expecting joy, calm, even renewal, but vulnerability and fear are sometimes key ingredients to getting there. I'm telling you this so you recognize fear when it appears, because at some point it will, and you may even feel like running. If this happens, stop yourself and remember I told you this would happen. You are wired for self-protection, yet there is no exploration, discovery, or journey without something that will make you feel uncomfortable. Make friends with those feelings, and realize they will stay in the journey with you: but examine what's really going on, and take those feelings for what they are worth.

Promise that...

You will get curious. Not just about the discovery and the journey, but your feelings, both in and out of the journey. You may think I'm making too big a deal about all these promises, but I'm just speaking from experience. As adults—especially women—we learn to suppress a lot. One of our greatest strengths is we are multi-taskers. We are also carriers and doers. We juggle a lot, physically, mentally, and emotionally for everyone in our individual spheres. We can't help it.

It is the way we are wired and even conditioned. And I believe one of our coping mechanisms is to suppress ourselves in the process.

This suppression that we have come to rely on doesn't serve us well, and if suppressed long enough, we will have to learn to cultivate our passions again. This suppression keeps us from making time for curiosity. The last person we consider is ourselves. You will say you never lost it. You are just too busy, or your kids demand too much. Your career is too overwhelming, or you don't have the mental energy for it. Believe me, you will use every excuse in the book, but I promise when you finally try to sit with it, you may be so out of practice that you feel uncomfortable. This is why I'm asking you to promise that you will get curious, because curiosity may just be the window into the things that cultivate the food for your soul that you need.

I find it helpful to create these promises for myself. The next activity allows you to state what I've mentioned above; and as you move through the exercise, I hope you will choose to actually make those promises to yourself. The beauty of putting this down on paper is it serves as an act of accountability. Give a copy to a close friend and ask them to hold you to it. Print this out and place it in a book or your journal or create a piece of art where you can put it on display. The very act of creating these promises will help you remember them when you get distracted or things get hard.

activity

Promise Activity

In this activity you will write a statement to yourself. This statement will be a promise that you personally draft to keep you on track and accountable during this process. Make it what you need it to be. Share it with an accountability partner, but whatever you do, don't break this promise to yourself.

I highly encourage you to include all the pieces on promises we just covered in the previous material. Maybe one area resonated with you more than another. Focus more attention there if you like. But just in case you need a place to get started, I have provided a template for you to use below.

I, _____, promise to approach my soul care journey with openness. I realize this exercise could take time, and I will need to listen to both my heart and head to move through the process of discovering what truly fuels my soul.

I also promise to not allow fear to lead. Just because at times I may feel vulnerable or even uncomfortable in this journey, this is not a reason to fear and discontinue my quest. It could be an opportunity to look deeper into myself and a reason to keep going.

Lastly, I promise to get curious. When I feel fear, I will get curious. When I find something interesting, I will explore it. When I feel a stirring in my soul, I will try it. I promise to use curiosity as my secret weapon.

Interludes

You may remember at the start of this book I mentioned interviews with other women on the topic of soul care. My purpose in sharing these stories is to show a variety of perspectives and experiences because I know we are all vastly different and coming at this from our own unique personalities and perspectives. My desire is that you might not only identify yourself in my story, but also see yourself in others. I have placed these stories sporadically throughout the book and called them interludes, so that as you explore what this topic means for you, you can identify with and discover truths through the experiences of other women.

"Finding joy in something
isn't full until you have felt
the bad."

Rebecca

Interlude

Rebecca's Story

I had the joy of speaking to a colleague, Rebecca, when I started on the journey of exploring what this book could be. I wanted to understand what other women feel, what they wrestle with, and if they struggle to find ways to nourish their souls.

My colleague was 28, recently divorced and had been in a really dark place during the prior year. While she and I did not work closely together, we had similar passions. She loved painting, art, photography, and music. She described walking outside and being with nature as an activity that brought her joy and nourished her soul. Interestingly, I didn't know we had these things in common before we sat down to chat.

When I pressed Rebecca on how these practices made her feel, she described these moments as moving and too hard to describe. She stated that they well up much emotion in her that being in the moment with them could cause her to cry. Her face lit up as she talked through what brought her tremendous joy, and I was thrilled to see that I was not the only one who experienced these feelings with activities that fueled my soul.

As in any conversation, you learn more and more the deeper you go. It shouldn't come as a surprise that her recent divorce came up in conversation. The pain we experience and process in our lives usually comes to the forefront. But I learned something powerful about Rebecca's pain. It was deep and raw. This meant that all the beautiful things that used to bring her joy lost their magic. She, in a sense, lost what was feeding her soul.

"Art had lost its purpose," Rebecca said. "I couldn't feel anything. Every activity came up void."

In the year after her divorce, she decided to take a year of self-care. She knew she needed to deal with this numbing emptiness. She decided to run straight into her challenges instead of running away from them, and she used a practice of self-care to move through them. What she discovered, though, was that she could no longer suppress her feelings. In order to get back to the magic, she had to "feel" the pain. It was the price to find balance and gratitude once again. She had pushed everything down so much that everything had lost feeling—even positive emotions.

Rebecca said, "You have to face the feelings—it's the worst and it's also the best when it actually gets you to the other side of your pain. Being able to find joy in something can't be felt until you have allowed yourself to feel the bad."

Rebecca's story is powerful because it is important for us to realize that we can't suppress our pain. If you are in a place where you struggle to find joy, let me encourage you to do the work. Run to your challenges; don't run away from them. Stop the suppressing, stop the pushing down, and allow yourself to feel your pain. This work is necessary in order for you to reach a place where your soul can actually be nourished. And I'm pretty confident you won't be able to discover what feeds your soul until it is done.

I experienced this in my own life. It was during my separation from my husband. It was excruciatingly painful, and if you have ever gone through something like this, you know. I remember sitting with my therapist, talking through all the dynamics. At the end of the conversation she said, "I have one thing I want you to do this week." I asked, "What is that?" She said, "I want you to go home and allow yourself to feel your pain." It was the last thing I wanted to do. My next question was "How?"

The "how" is the hard part. The "how" is what we avoid. The "how" for me looked like sobbing, naked for hours in the dark in my bathtub. And that was just the start. That "how" looked like a couple of years of hard work not only to process my grief, but also to move forward in my relationship with my husband. The "how" -- it is difficult, but you have to feel the pain before you can conquer it.

I think about it like this: when you are at a place where nothing brings you joy and your soul is malnourished, it's like a cancer has taken over your ability to digest your food. You lose your appetite, then you don't feed yourself. You have to do something drastic, maybe even surgical. You may require a special diet and even a lot of rest. It's going to hurt, but the work to feel the negative feelings and emotions must be done in order to move to a place where you can be nourished. Your suppression avoids the painful work, but if you do it, I promise it will be worth it. Maybe not in one day, maybe not even in a year, but you will eventually come out of it, and you will find that joy again.

It's okay to feel the bad. It may just unlock this powerful world that lies before you.

6

Do You Know Who You Are

You may remember that in the introduction I stated that I believe that what feeds our souls is as deeply a part of us as our DNA. It is part of our wiring and I believe we are created special and unique. Why wouldn't the things that feed our souls show up in the same way?

This is why I believe it is important that women understand who they are. Without this knowledge, it would have been hard for me to connect the dots in discovering what actually nourished my soul. In this next section I give a few ideas; but discovering yourself is a very personal journey. My suggestion here is to see this area not necessarily as a "how to" but as a place to start. The hope is that the more you search, the more you will uncover the various pieces of yourself that can potentially unlock what feeds you.

Personality Assessments

When I polled over 50 women and asked, "Do you know who you are?" the response was a resounding "Yes." Everyone seemed to believe she knew who she was. They had filled out a myriad of personality assessments, and yet almost 84% admitted they didn't quite know what to do with them.

I find people either love these assessments or hate them. I personally find them helpful, and I also encourage folks when they can, to hire a career coach to help them go deeper in understanding these specific pieces of themselves. But I'm not sure we generally think about these assessments when it comes to learning how to take care of ourselves—I know I didn't. Knowledge is power, and there are nuggets in these assessments that can help cultivate those passions that live deep within you.

I share this information because I believe personality assessments can be a tool. They are not the only way to discover what feeds your soul, but I do believe the more you know about yourself, the better able you are to understand how you are wired. Somewhere in that wiring is what fuels your soul. My suggestion here is to look at these personality assessments as a way to get to know yourself a little better. Understanding my personality didn't uncover what would fuel me, but it did help me understand a little bit behind why certain things fed me and other things didn't. Sometimes just understanding this can help you avoid an area that isn't going to work for you.

For example, I'm a Meyers Briggs ENFJ type: Extroverted, Intuitive, Feeling and Judging. Without going too deep into what all of this means, I will focus on the extroverted/introverted traits because most people are generally familiar with these. I originally thought that being extroverted meant that I was energized by being with people. This is true, but there are times when being with people can feel draining. I asked my career coach about this, and she said, "Being extroverted doesn't necessarily mean that you only derive your energy from being around other people. It also means that you derive energy from stimulating things around you." This puzzled me a bit until I talked to an introverted friend, and she shared her favorite way to receive energy, "It's in the dark, in my bed, and all alone for hours." Yeah, not the same.

This was a stark contrast because as she shared that, something visceral welled up inside of me. I need a LOT of stimulation—like nature, art, atmosphere, culture, and travel and I enjoy it most when I am with someone.

Here is how I think you could potentially apply this to your own discovery. Use what you learn about your personality to ask yourself why certain activities work for you and why some don't. Ask this in your work and in your daily activities. You will see the connection to your personality and begin to identify what gives you energy. For me, these pieces of my personality help me understand that burying my head in research over a topic will most likely be draining for me, while this is stimulating for my sister, who is an introvert.

Again, the assessments, in my opinion, won't necessarily define what you need to feed your soul. They may just give you a little direction or even explain why some things resonate with you and others don't. If you would like to learn more, here are some of my favorite resources on various ways you can dissect your own personality type:

Meyers-Briggs

Enneagram

DISC

7

Understanding How What You Do Doesn't Make You Who You Are

What we do in many ways defines us. I think we can get pretty wrapped up in it–so much so that we can start believing that entirely external person is who we are. What we do may be a piece of who we are, but it isn't necessarily our whole person; and sometimes what we do can make us forget who we are.

Ah, did I get caught in this trap! Whether you are in a career, retired, raising children, single or married, many of us can lump all these descriptors together and expect satisfaction from them, and maybe even meaning. I also believe many of us rattle off mom, wife, sister, or friend when we go to describe ourselves. I don't know about you, but I don't usually start with my "day job." My first thought isn't, "I'm a marketer." But when you enter into a conversation with someone new, ironically being a mom, wife, or sister doesn't even come up at first. I generally mention my career.

Here's what I mean. One of the first questions you will ask or get asked when you meet someone new is "What do you do?" Now, if you are a stay-at-home mom, this might come up in the conversation, but the first thing we focus on is what we do for work. I'm a marketer. You are a therapist, doctor, teacher, nurse, lawyer, stay-at-home mom, etc. A good bit of who we believe we are is wrapped up in what we do for a living, but I want to caution you here. What you need to feed your soul may not be present in the work you do every day. Heck, there may be nothing about your career or day-to-day activities that points to what fuels your soul. And that isn't necessarily a problem. It's just life.

I challenge this idea that what we do equals who we are because I do believe that even if you do something you love, there still may be a need to nourish your soul. I bring this up because for the longest time I looked to my career as the place where I should be able to find satisfaction, even joy. My career was the thing that should fuel me, right? Then why was I generally frustrated?

You may wonder why I looked to my job. It was because I think we have been sold that our work should fuel our passions. I'm not saying that they shouldn't, but I think we have a lot of romantic notions about what this means or what this should feel like. Work is work. It has deadlines, stress, and expectations and is completely tied to our compensation. If things go south, you can lose your job, and many of us are constantly thinking about how we get to the next thing or the next level.

I think we make up these romantic notions about a lot of things, such as ministry, motherhood, and even volunteerism. This doesn't mean that magical fulfillment can't exist in my work, but I realized I was expecting these magical feelings to show up there, and they weren't. Later I would realize I was looking at everything backwards. Getting paid for my passions wasn't necessarily my end game. I mean, it could eventually be, but I would still need to feed my soul. This is when I realized that feeding my soul is essential to my being able to do my best in whatever I am doing—career, home, ministry, friendships--all of it. Looking to work to provide that fulfillment only made me frustrated and discontented.

Let's face it, not all of us get to do what we are passionate about, and there are seasons that result in different paths (like potty training my toddlers—need I say more?). Finances also play a role. Some of us are just starting out, and I rarely find a person who is completely passionate about his or her work when they are at the beginning of their careers. The "do what you love, and you will never work a day in your life" mentality is not the reality for most of us, and it isn't because we aren't pursuing our passions. It can take a lot of time to earn the professional capital to get it. And yet, what we do much of the time is how we define ourselves.

As I started looking to my career for this kind of fulfillment, I was able to do a little research using the personality assessments I mentioned previously. I felt it was important to understand what drove me. I discovered through a series of assessments that I am driven by influence and creativity. If I have those two pieces, I'm "sure" to find fulfillment.

What is interesting is that my job in marketing for a big brand brought me serious influence and opportunities for creativity, but not in the way I was wanting it. I thought I wanted to make creative assets, develop campaigns, work with various designers, do photoshoots, you name it. But that didn't happen, and I was just close enough to it that it almost made me frustrated. The work I was asked to do involved a great deal of influence and problem-solving, which allowed me to get creative, but not in a visual way that I enjoyed.

But here's the thing, I did love these aspects about my job. I love a hard challenge that requires me to figure something out and rally groups to our end goal. I love this so much I've wondered if I need therapy because the messier the problem is and the more people it takes to bring together, the more excited I get about it. But this work was still leaving a void.

I also knew enough from my creative background that creating for others is not always what it is cracked up to be because there are boundaries, standards, and consistency needed to perpetuate a brand visually. I started to understand that I love the freedom to create visually but in my own way.

But this is what had me stumped: if the need for visual creativity was such a part of me, then how was it going to come to life? Turns out, it really comes to life in everything I do. All creativity is fun to me, but that visual, autonomous creativity that is not confined to the standards, principles, and boundaries of a brand is what I needed to fuel my soul. I was looking for the magic in all the wrong places. The magic wasn't in my work; it was found in the places where I could create in an uninhibited manner, answerable only to myself.

I still use influence and creativity in my job every day. I still identify myself as a marketer for the brand that I work for. But I no longer look to it as a way to fuel my soul.

Don't get me wrong, some of you get to do exactly what you love doing for your work. And if you are lucky enough to make money pursuing the thing that you are the most passionate about, I'm sure you will agree that there is some form of that thing that you have to hold dear for yourself. If you don't, there is something that seems to get lost in the pursuit of "something," whether that is fame, fortune, influence, or money.

Not looking to my career for fulfillment is a principle I wish I had realized when I was a creative entrepreneur. I had a small business that I built from nothing. I designed personalized notecards for friends and family, and I started to think I could sell them. It turned out, I could, and people loved the personalization piece of my business. My tagline was, "It's great to do what one loves." And I did, indeed, love it. But I also wore every hat. We had no money. I did all the design, production, packaging, and shipment. I did the bookkeeping, customer service, product photography, public relations pitches, and much more, all while taking care of my Irish twins full time.

I would get up early and answer customer inquiries, take care of the kids when they woke up; then while they would play or nap, I would cut and fulfill orders. We would run to the post office (among all the other errands), move into the witching hour, have dinner and baths, and then I'd sit on the floor while my husband and I watched TV together and I cut and filled more orders. I worked a TON of hours, and my little business grew. It grew and grew and grew to the point where five years later, I was completely burned out.

One of my mistakes looking back is that I didn't keep a creative practice for myself. It was always about producing the next thing to make a buck--coming up with the next big idea or meeting a sales goal I had for myself. I no longer had the juice left to take my business to the next level, and the last thing I wanted to do was create the things that I once loved.

Even when our passions are found in our day-to-day work, we still must keep something sacred. We must schedule and cultivate those sacred practices to feed our souls. I'm not saying to not look at your career or vocation when searching for what this might be. Just be

understanding how what you do doesn't make you who you are

aware that a big part of how you may understand yourself could be wrapped up in what you do (or don't do) for a living. There may be clues there, but my guess is if you are here, you are tired. If you have identified that you need to cultivate better practices of self-care, then looking at your work for fulfillment probably isn't going to cut it right now. I encourage you to dive deeper into what really connects you to the things you love and why.

I hope that sharing some of these fundamental pieces has been helpful for you to start evaluating and understanding where you may need to start finding your own nourishment. And since we have gotten this piece out of the way, I want to ask you an important question: do you know what you love?

8

Do You Know What You Love

This is the question that most people get stumped on. You might find that puzzling, but when I ask someone if there is an activity or practice that totally lights them up and gives them this magic that I have described in these pages, most cannot answer me immediately. It takes a minute and some thinking to answer, and some get totally stumped. Why? Because (1) They have never experienced what I am talking about or (2) They haven't really thought about it before.

Most of us are just going through the day-to-day motions, and I personally couldn't answer this question either before I did this work. Not the deep question about magic. I would probably be reading these pages thinking that the author was some kind of whacko until I experienced it. I would have thought that you couldn't find that kind of feeling in an activity–something spiritual, beautiful, and magical all rolled up into one. And who has time for it anyway?

My list would have consisted of all the things many of my friends mentioned. I love travel, spa days, coffee with friends, shopping, and girls' trips. But my self-care consisted of checking out much more than I was even doing these things, arguably because they involved people, time, and money. I don't know about you, but at the end of the day I'm ready to go home and put on my pajamas and crawl into bed. I just don't have a ton of energy to give to something "extra."

Even when I was taking the time to "take care" of myself, it wasn't in these favorite activities. It was on social media, binge-watching Netflix, and getting on social media again. A spa day, while enjoyable, would come up short, and I always craved more time with my girlfriends. It was never enough.

I thought I knew what I liked to do, but I had no idea what actually was feeding my soul. I knew what I enjoyed doing to check out, but I never put into practice things that continually filled me up. And this begs the question, how do you discover what you love?

"If I didn't have these things [activities that nourished her soul] in my life, I'd die just a little bit every single day."

Elizabeth

Interlude

Elizabeth's Story

Elizabeth is the type of woman from the outside that many try to emulate as they marvel at her ability to juggle career, family, health, and spirituality. I personally found her intimidating until I happened to get to travel with her on a three-hour car ride back from a conference. She is intense, passionate, and sound in her convictions.

She is wicked smart too, which was also one of the reasons I was probably intimidated by her in the beginning. I knew my interview with her would yield clear thoughts and wisdom that could either unnerve me or inspire me (and I mean that in the sincerest, most wonderful way). Elizabeth has a way of helping you dig just a little deeper and look at something from an entirely different perspective.

I also wanted to interview Elizabeth because, unlike me, she is a disciplined person. I kind of thought that if anyone could debunk my hunch, it was her.

As predicted, she brought her full self to the conversation. I knew discipline would play a part, but as I began to ask her about what truly fueled her, she was quick to respond. She said, "it's two and a half things." Curious, I asked what they were?

I was not surprised when exercise played a role. Elizabeth is faithful in the gym and in her diet, which I know contributes to her cute little figure. I've certainly been envious of her discipline and the results that come from it. But ironically, exercise fell into the "half." I think she knew I would know this answer because she made a point to say that it fueled her, but it wasn't the only thing. Public speaking and helping people develop a business were two pieces of her life that bring joy to her soul.

These activities being so different from my own, I asked, "So how do these things make you feel?" She answered, "Doing these things involves all of me. I get so wrapped up in the moment, in that activity, that I don't even need basic human needs. I don't think about eating or rest. I'm all in, and I love every minute of it."

I was interested in getting to the heart of the emotion for her. I wanted to be open that these feelings may be different for each person, I asked, "what would you feel if these things went away?" Her response was immediate. She said, "if I didn't have these things in my life, I'd die just a little bit every single day."

This was powerful for me to hear. She would "die just a little bit every single day." Do we think about the things we love in this way? Are we practicing them in such a way that we recognize the life they are giving us? If you aren't there yet, I believe you can get there.

What's interesting is that any emotions of feeling stuck, frustrated, and even trapped are evidence of you "dying just a little more each day" because you haven't discovered or fostered the needs of your soul. This nourishment for Elizabeth gave her life. She has discovered that her existence--her showing up well and her joy--are tied to these practices in her life, and she now looks at her personal and professional life in ways that foster these practices. She not only knows they are gifts, but she has recognized how they play a role in her satisfaction. She understands that when she doesn't do these things, she doesn't show up to her career, her family, and her relationships in the best way.

Elizabeth says, "I've learned that these pieces have to be a part. I've talked to my manager at work, and my husband even understands my need to take a weekend to speak at a conference when asked because he, like me, knows that the joy it brings me actually makes me a better person."

- - - - - - - - - - -

Discovering what you love can be easy for some and difficult for others, but a key ingredient to this discovery is curiosity. Remember those little promises I asked you to make in the beginning? It's time to leverage them. Remember that fear may accompany the openness and curiosity you have promised to hold dear, but you have also promised not to allow fear to hold you back.

I believe that it is through pursuing curiosity and being open that you can find what you love. You can do this a lot of different ways, but let me tell you about one of my favorites. It's called making a date with yourself.

9

Dating Yourself

Yep! You heard me correctly. Have you ever had a date with yourself? It may sound funny, but if you are a woman, you probably haven't given yourself much permission to spend time all by your lonesome. I mean, many of us mothers can't even go to the bathroom without interruption.

Here is what I want you to know. This is not necessarily THE way you will find what feeds you, but it is A way, and it works for me quite regularly. It works so much so that I now set up these times at least on a yearly basis.

If you are intrigued, here is what I want you to do. If you are interested in using this tactic to help discover what could nourish you, set an appointment on your calendar and spend the day with yourself. Introverts, you are probably jumping for joy. Extroverts, you may be thinking, what am I going to do for a full day by myself? Let me be the first extrovert to tell you, you can do this and actually enjoy it.

Here is how it works. I encourage both introverts and extroverts to choose a location you are excited about. It cannot be at your home, in your bed, under your covers, or where a friend meets you for lunch. For my first date with myself, I found a lovely spot near my home where I could spend all day at a coffee shop, walk the grounds when I needed a break, step into a shop just to see what they offered, grab a bit of lunch nearby, and take a hike later that afternoon or walk through a design home tour. It was sublime.

It was something I really looked forward to, and after I did it, I decided to try to make it a yearly occurrence. But I used this time to ask myself a lot of questions. Some were focused on personal development, but the other piece of it was to cultivate activities that I wanted to pursue in the next year. These activities were simply a list of things about which I at some point had thought, "that seems interesting to me. I think I would enjoy trying that." If you haven't even had time to think that far, then consider just googling "fun things to do in your spare time" or "top ten activities for extroverts/introverts" and see what comes up.

This is not a complicated science, and like I said, it may result in you finding something you love.

Another way to start generating a list is to remember back to when you were young—what sports or activities did you enjoy? Or better yet, what activity did you want to try but you never got the opportunity to. You can even think about subjects you loved in school. Think back to times over your life where you can remember sparks of joy or gratitude. All of these things are indicators and can get those juices flowing on ideas to pursue.

For me, when I first started, I made a really long list—more like 20. I did this because it was the first time I had really given myself the time to think about it. After I looked at the list, I then determined to figure out which few I'd actually get serious about.

dating yourself

Here's the thing: you will need to get realistic with yourself. You may want to do all 20 things, but will you? I find that my success and satisfaction generally is better when I get honest about what I am able to do. For me, I try to limit it to three to five things. I know that five is really pushing it for me (yes, even within a year). I generally try to stick with three (with the other two in the wings just in case I can make it work later in the year).

Now, for some of you, this is all you need to do: make a list and whittle it down to what generates the most interest or stirring in your soul. That stirring is a pretty good sign you might be on to something. For others, it might not be that easy. You may still do this exercise and come up short. This is when you need to foster your curiosity.

What I recommend is that you use some of the time you have designated in your day date and do some research. What excites you when you read about it? Where do you have to go to do it? What is the cost going to look like, and is there a good time of year to do it? Once you have narrowed down your list, set two more dates with yourself on your calendar to experience whatever it is you fancy. Then get to planning, scheduling, saving, or whatever it is that you need to do. Do it and stick to it.

If you are wondering what a list might look like, I'll share the one I made for this year:

Paddle boarding
Sailing
Hot tea - learning about and sampling
Watercolor
Visiting a monastery

Learning more about contemplative prayer
Attending a Buddhist meeting on meditation
Hiking a local park in the city
Learning from a friend who put together a coffee table book
Looking through Domino Magazine
Walking a labyrinth
Taking a candle-making class

It's all over the place, but I'm interested in all these things. After I did this little exercise, I decided to shift these things around. As I worked through, I realized I wanted some of these things for myself, some I'm not as interested in, some I'd prefer to do with others or my family, and some are small enough to tackle whenever. Here is an example of how I broke it up:

Revised List
Date with myself
Watercolor class
Visit a monastery
Attend a Buddhist meeting on meditation

Date with hubs
Paddle boarding

Read
Book on contemplative prayer - research
Domino Magazine

With the fam
Hike in the city at a local park
Candle-making class with my daughter

Once I'm done, I will hold on to my original list for the next year's date. I'll do this process again and reevaluate the list from the last year to see if I'm still interested in some of the things I didn't accomplish. Again, this will look different for everyone, but now you at least have something you are intentionally going to go after. And guess what, if you hate the activity or find that it doesn't feed your soul, you know.

I think approaching any of these activities with a sense of adventure is really important. If you come to it with openness, then it is harder for disappointment to settle in. Even if it doesn't bring you the magic you were hoping for, you tried it and now you know.

Also, as you move through this process, hold yourself with some grace. There may be some things on your list that you aren't even sure why you are interested in them. You may struggle with changing them because you feel like other activities are more "normal" or "cool" or others would find them more interesting. Let me remind you that you promised to stay open and get curious. We are going to talk about fear in a little bit too, but don't let your discomfort or vulnerability get in your way.

I have to ward off these things as well. I want to learn to paddle board (or at least try it), but I'm afraid it might be too hard or I'll embarrass myself and fall off. My interest in a Buddhist meeting on meditation makes me nervous because my religion is different. For me, learning about the activities, customs, and teachings of another religion is helpful in both understanding others different from myself, but also in affirming my own faith. I want to learn, but I almost struck it from my list because I feared what others may think of me (which is why it made the list).

Openness also means that you have to hold these ideas or activities open. I love the visual of holding something. When we hold something tightly it stays put. When we open our hands upward, holding the item with open palms, it can be kept, given, or even fall away. Making this list does not mean that you have to do any of it again after you try it. If it doesn't bring you joy, then keep exploring.

Once you have created your list (whether done in a 30-minute session with yourself or over a day date), you have to go do it. Plan that activity and try it. Be sure to take note of how you feel throughout the activity, and I highly encourage you to schedule some time afterwards to ask yourself a few questions:

1. Would I do this again? If so, why?
2. What would I change about it? What would I keep the same?
3. How did this activity feel in the moment?
4. Did I lose track of time or find myself feeling joyful or excited while I was performing this activity? Did it stir my soul?
5. How did it make me feel afterwards—the same, drained, or energized? Did I feel refreshed?
6. Did I wake up thinking about it the next day or within the week? Did I have thoughts like, "I can't wait to do that again?"
7. Would you be sad if you were told you could never do this activity again?

If you can answer most of these things in the positive, then I would encourage you to start prioritizing these activities and see what happens. Your interest may fizzle out quickly, or you may find, like I did, that it unlocks something for you that is both beautiful and nourishing for your soul.

Here is the thing, it may or may not spark magic for you at the start. It also may absolutely blow you away. But my recommendation is to keep approaching this topic and journey with openness, curiosity, vulnerability, and little expectation; and remember, none of this time is wasted. It's okay to let an activity fall away. Keep exploring, and I bet if you are curious or open enough, you will start to find the things that nourish your soul purely because you are approaching your journey with intentionality. Remember, I believe we all have something that can nourish our souls. Many of us just haven't given ourselves the time to think about it, much less discover it.

activity

Day Date Worksheet

Use the below to plan and execute your day date. You can start filling it out before you go or use this as a place to start.

place

_____

_____

_____

date

_____

_____

On a separate piece of paper, list activities that you are interested in trying. Don't think too hard about what they are--just make a list. If necessary, set a timer for 3-5 minutes and write as many things as you can think of. Once you have created that list, go back through and highlight or circle 5-10 activities you want to explore or research during your time today. List those here.

_____

_____

_____

_____

_____

_____

_____

_____

_____

_____

_____

_____

_____

Now, transfer the top 3-5 things you want to pursue below. State why you want to try this activity and what you hope to learn.

_____

_____

_____

_____

_____

_____

_____

_____

_____

_____

_____

_____

These worksheets can be found in a workbook available at www. alisonenglish.com/resources.

"I wonder if soul care doesn't look this way for everyone. I'm not sure I have ever felt this way about anything before."

Charnelle

Interlude

Charnelle's Story

When Charnelle committed to sit down with me to discuss the topic of self-care, she admitted that she may not have much to offer the conversation. I assured her that the intention was less her sharing specifically what she thought on the subject and more to hear her personal thoughts and experiences in general on the topic.

I don't think either one of us had real expectations of what would come out of our time together. That's generally how I tried to approach these interviews. I truly wanted to see what would organically come out of the conversation. I intentionally didn't plant seeds prior to the meeting because my goal was to see how women felt about the topic and learn, genuinely, about their experiences with it.

Charnelle is a young professional. Our worlds collided while working on that really large project I described at the start of this book. We spent a lot of time together, and I think we both quickly realized that despite our differences in race, marital status, and age, we were kindred spirits.

As with many of my friends, she is really smart and comes with big city (New York to be exact) chops in the public relations world.

I was impressed by her early on. She is poised, beautiful, and has a wardrobe I envy. Charnelle presents herself with confidence—a confidence I wish I had at her age. But the more I got to know her, I knew her professional talents were coupled with a sincere kindness and love for others.

As we sat down to discuss self-care practices, she spoke of time reading, Bible study, and time with friends. As a single person, community is a big part of how she cares for herself. She also spoke of the recent adoption of her dog, a new companion since she lives alone.

But after I described to her what soul care is, what it feels like, and how I believe it shows up, her immediate response was, "I wonder if soul care doesn't look this way for everyone. I'm not sure I have ever felt this way about anything before." Now, I could have been discouraged. I knew that I could be totally wrong about my theory, and that is okay. Guess what? I agreed with her. There is a large probability that not everyone will feel this way or have an activity that refuels them in the way I have described here.

As with any of my interviews, we continued talking. Because I wanted an organic conversation, I generally just asked a series of questions determined entirely by the course of the conversation. At some point in the interview, I must have referenced something that struck Charnelle in such a way that she immediately switched gears. I couldn't even tell you what I asked or even said, but she had a revelation. She said, "I think I know something that I could describe this way."

"What is it?" I asked

"It is deejaying," she said.

I smiled and asked her why. "When I was living in New York City,

I decided to take this up. As a child, music was a large part of my upbringing, and early on I discovered a love for it. I promised myself when I moved here [Atlanta] that I would take some classes and devote some time to it. I just haven't made the time. I actually forgot about it."

Now, I was thinking deejaying, that's pretty cool, but I wanted to know, why was it hard for her to realize this might be one of the things that fuels her? I asked her. Charnelle said, "As you were talking, I started thinking back to things in my childhood that I knew made me happy, joyful even. Music was always one of them. I loved making playlists and as I got older, I met some people who either deejayed on the side or for a living. They were amazing, and it drew me in. I decided to explore it. I even tried it out and every time I did it, I had so much fun. It took me thinking back to my childhood to make the connection, and now I'm asking myself why I haven't taken it up in the two years I have lived here."

This was really interesting to me, and I wish I had thought of this before. I think there is a lot to learn about what we love. Much of it can be found in the haunts of our past. It can come to life differently as an adult or it can come to life in the same way. Elizabeth Gilbert writes about this in her book *Big Magic*. A friend of hers found life again in returning to her roots of ice skating. It was something she loved as a child but then let pass by for a myriad of reasons—time, her ability, the fact that she was grown. When she rediscovered her love of it, she started incorporating it into her schedule on a regular basis, and it brought joy to her life. She wasn't looking to skate professionally; she was looking to exercise her love of skating to bring her personal joy.

My time with Charnelle helped me discover that our past can tell us a lot about our present. Our past joys can also direct us towards activities that can and will feed our souls. If you are still stumped after doing your day date or asking yourself the long list of questions I posed to you earlier, revisit your childhood. Ask, what was I passionate about? What activity brought me a joy? My friend, those young, uninhibited years may just be the thing to help you define what to get curious about again. It may unlock this idea of soul care for you.

section 3

Connection to
Spirituality

10

Faith and Feeding Your Soul

"My soul, wait in silence for God only, for my hope is from Him."
Psalm 62:5 (NASB)

Look up the definition of the word "soul" on the internet and you will find a myriad of definitions, but most point to the spiritual being of an individual. Now if you don't believe that humans are immortal, you may just want to skip this chapter; but if you feel there is something that exists beyond the human body like I do, please read on because this may just change your life.

Remember the reference to the soul in the beginning of this book? "The soul is defined as the principle of life, feeling, thought, and action in humans, regarded as a distinct entity separate from the body, and commonly held to be separable in existence from the body; the spiritual part of humans as distinct from the physical part. The spiritual part of humans regarded in its moral aspect, or as believed to survive death and be subject to happiness or misery in a life to come" (*dictonary.com*). Since I believe that humans are immortal and live beyond their physical body, it should come as no surprise that I see a strong connection between this practice of feeding one's soul and one's faith.

I am no theologian, and you could argue that maybe I discovered this wonderful insight out of vain pursuit, but I know that God found me in the practice. You see, I grew up as a fundamentalist Christian. My view of God was somewhat tyrannical. It was fraught with rules and guilt, steeped in tradition, and checking boxes for what a holy, righteous, and good person should be. But what it lacked was any notion that the Christian life left me free, grateful, or even joyful. I was taught to spend hours in prayer and learn passages of Scripture. Christianity was all about following rules, rules, and more rules. To be a good Christian meant to avoid "self" and rid anything outside of the "rules" from my life.

For a creative person like myself, this did not embody joy. It was restrictive. Holiness did not have an expression other than the following of rules to earn God's favor, and it was flat-out boring. It wasn't beautiful. There was no magic, worship, or overwhelming love, and I felt an immense guilt over just about everything in my life. My relationship with God felt toxic, like an obligation.

Some would argue, if you believe Christ died for your sins and freed you from everlasting damnation, isn't that beautiful? My answer is yes, but if you believe that it exists with this attitude of earning, obligation, and drudgery, this belief becomes conditional—not about God's love for me—and there is no beauty in that.

It's no surprise that my relationship with God struggled. Most of us would tell our friends to get out of a relationship like that with another human being, and it is one of the reasons I believe many people leave their faith. God, to me, represented something big and scary, not fun or loving. He felt distant, and I didn't believe that He found delight in me.

I would read Scriptures like, "Take delight in the Lord and He will give you the desires of your heart" (Psalm 37:4). In all honesty, if this experience was my way to delight in the Lord, I wasn't really digging it. And how could the desires of my heart be holy and righteous if I was to avoid self? Was I living a lie?

I was six when I became a Christian, and if you have grown up in your faith, whatever that may be, you eventually have to make a decision as an adult (maybe a few times over) that you do, indeed, believe it. I'm grateful that the faith I live today looks different from the faith I was brought up in. It is beautiful, challenging, and gracious--a life of freedom, worship, and grace. It is both holy and real. It is reverent and whimsical, and it is magic.

It's been a journey for me to get here, but the crux of my faith shifted when I discovered that God was in the magic of feeding my soul. The Bible teaches that we are made in God's image. If we are made in His image and He lives in us, then that means that our beings are connected deeply to who He is. He has created us to be who we are, and He has created us as creators because He is the ultimate Creator.

When you discover who you are and what you love, know that God gave that to you. When you nourish your soul and it brings you joy, He did that for you. That passion, the love, the overwhelming sense you get from doing something that fuels your soul—God did that for you.

These activities, as I have stated before, are tied to the way we are wired. At their purest sense, they are God coming alive in each of us, and He is meeting us there in that moment, showering us with

His love. I believe the experience of feeding one's soul is one of the closest things to worship we can fully understand and experience, and it will take your breath away. It's a tangible way for you to take delight in your heavenly Father and how He shows delight in you. If you want to feel free, experience joy, and express worship, just pursue this idea; and I promise you, you will feel the presence of God in your life.

For me, this comes to life in the flow of painting and in the daily rituals as well—lighting a candle, walking through a park, noticing the dew on a tree bough, sipping my morning cup of coffee or quiet meditation. They are all gifts, and they are ways in which God tells me just how much He loves me. It's beautiful.

And just as this spiritual sense is heightened with the regular digestion of my soul care, I have begun to discover that the benefits of feeding my soul overflow into spiritual practices that I always found an obligation. They no longer feel stale. Scripture has taken on new life. Prayer feels more personal. Being still and clearing my mind allows me to feel God's presence in deeper ways. And my worship, both in person and in a corporate setting, has unfolded in a way I never experienced in my youth.

You know what I know without a doubt? My God, He delights in me. I no longer live a life of guilt, but one fully wrapped in the love of my Father who shows me every day that He loves me. God is in this type of nourishment. He created it. He wired you for it, and He will use it to show you just how much He loves you. Now, go and be fed.

section 4

What Gets in the Way

"I had to learn that it was okay that I wasn't wired or created to want to be all of those things [traditional persona of a woman]. I suffered with feeling selfish for years until I learned it was okay. I let it go and leaned into my wiring, and there was so much freedom."

Brittany

Interlude

Brittany's Story

My friend, Brittany, has one of those vivacious personalities that is contagious. When we get together, our conversations are fun, and productive. You can go deep with her without feeling like you are really going there. There is a bright, happy energy she brings to every conversation. I always leave our time together feeling uplifted and recharged—what a gift, right?

I've also never met someone with the ability to connect people and things like she can. We have this in common, but Brittany takes it to another level. It's an important thing to note about her in relation to this topic because it's a big piece of how she fuels her soul.

She was excited to talk to me about this topic and warned me up front: "I'm probably not like most women. All the things you are describing, they aren't me. This whole thing about nurturing or care, feeling like I have to carry everyone and everything, I don't think about it. If I need to care for myself, I do it."

For a moment, I thought, well, there it is, my theory is debunked. But I wanted to see where the conversation would go because she was passionate about the topic, and I knew she always has something enlightening to say. I also think it is important to share this because you may actually be like Brittany, and my goal is to represent a wide variety of women, their passions, and their experiences with things that feed their soul.

But where I had an "aha" within Brittany's story was in the journey it took her to recognize this in herself. You see, Brittany realized several years ago that she didn't "feel" like other women. She was raised in a small town where women became teachers or nurses so that they could be more available for their children. She followed in these footsteps and chose teaching as a profession. She taught for one year and was miserable. She started asking herself, "What is wrong with me?"

She had several stages of discovery finding that this innate, traditional, nurturing quality seemed non-existent in her. It seemed like something was wrong. When she became a mom, she struggled through every day of her maternity leave. "I loved my son, but I felt trapped. I couldn't wait to get back to work," she said. "I would look at my friends, Pinterest, Instagram, and would think, why am I struggling? This is supposed to be one of the most meaningful times in my life, right? Aren't I supposed to enjoy being home with my baby? Look at what all these wonderful mothers are doing." But she felt miserable. What they were doing was the last thing she wanted to do. She felt ashamed and selfish.

She discovered an ironic connection in her journey as she struggled through her feelings and lack of nurturing responses. In her college years during the first year of her marriage, she was tasked to do a research paper on any topic she wanted in one of her psychology classes. She picked one that resonated with her and it took her down a road of self-discovery.

She had a big "aha" and decided to work with a therapist after finishing her paper. She started realizing that she had a good bit of memory blockage from her childhood. She couldn't recall memories like friends and family could. Her memories were based on pictures (which she thought was normal), but nothing else. She didn't realize people had memories without needing a picture to recall that time.

And this was puzzling: why did she literally have years of child-hood that were blocked? After some discussion with her family, she discovered she did have some trauma as a child and didn't have any memory of it. She had blocked it all and, with that, many other things were blocked as well. Through therapy she was able to connect the dots between this trauma and some of how she was wired.

Who is to say if Brittany's wiring would have been different had she not experienced this in her life? The reality is that there are a lot of things that create our wiring. There is good, bad, our DNA, our personalities, and many varying circumstances. Who we are is shaped by all these things.

When Brittany got to adulthood and put on the persona that all women are told we should be, she found it didn't fit, and she felt broken. But what came out of a painful journey is something quite beautiful. She finally accepted who she really was.

What I love about this is we are all told our role as women is a lot of things. Brené Brown in her book *Daring Greatly* talks about this. "In a US study on conformity to feminine norms, researchers recently listed the most important attributes associated with being feminine as being nice, pursuing a thin body ideal, showing modesty by not calling attention to one's talents or abilities , being domestic, caring for children, investing in a romantic relationship, keeping sexual in-timacy contained within one committed relationship, and using our resources to invest in our appearances" (pg. 89).

This is what we are told to be. This is who we believe we must be in order to become good, successful mothers, partners, and friends. And this may not be who you are at all. As Brittany discovered, many of these things just weren't her.

But where she struggled and failed to step into her true authentic self was in the area of comparison—something we as women tend to struggle with. Brittany said her comparison to other women was bad. She started realizing that she had to quit following many women on Instagram. "I would watch their stories, see their feeds, and it would be a constant reminder to me that I don't measure up—or at least that is how I looked at it then. I know I'm not the room mom. I'm not going to have balloons and cupcakes for my kids when they wake up on their birthday. I don't care if I cook a meal for my family and I hire a tutor to help my boys with schoolwork because it totally and absolutely drains me. I love working, and I don't feel an ounce of guilt about taking time for myself," she said. "I would much rather do what I am doing today than be on maternity leave or home with my kids full time," which is a full-time graduate student, managing a demanding, full-time career, mom of two busy boys, and married to a great hubby who travels.

It all stems back to what really fuels her soul: curiosity. Brittany discovered that she thrives when she is able to ideate and learn. She calls it a variation of exposure. I call it ferocious curiosity.

"I had to learn that it was okay that I wasn't wired or created to want to be all of those things. I suffered with feeling selfish for years until I learned it was okay. I let it go and leaned into my wiring, and there was so much freedom," she said. And her family life flourished.

"I may not be room mom, but I show up in other ways," says

Brittany. And ironically, they are connected back to her wiring. "I'm active with my kids. I focus on the quality of my time with them. We play a lot more; I put my phone away. When we talk, I'm sitting eye to eye, curious and listening. When we play, I'm all in—experiencing the moment with them, playing ball in the yard, nerf gun wars across the house, discovering, connecting with them," Brittany said. "In my mind, being a good mom doesn't mean that I have to make dinner. For me, outsourcing dinner means that I get to spend more time with my boys. I've accepted this about myself and we are all better for it. In the end, my kids don't care if I made their dinner. They don't know any different, but they will remember my intentional time with them, and that really matters to me."

Brittany also talked about how accepting her wiring not only made her family life flourish, but she also let go of unrealistic expectations in her marriage. "My husband and I love to talk and connect. We go deep on what we are learning, and we love to talk about business. We laugh A LOT and have fun together. Ironically, he never put the 'normal' expectations of being a 'good wife' on me, but I did. I found I was able to enjoy my relationship much more when I let go of comparison and leaned into who I am. I showed up as my authentic self in my relationship with him, and it made a world of difference."

It's obvious that this variation of exposure plays a beautiful role in her relationship with her boys and her husband. She sees the gift that it is now, embracing it *vs* trying to be something she isn't.

"Here's the thing," Brittany said, "I can't help but seek out this variation of exposure for myself or even with others. I love connecting people, articles, and conversations and bringing them all together. It's why I believe I prefer being in grad school with all these responsibilities to cuddling with my newborn during maternity leave. I get this crazy amount of energy from it because I'm actually living into who I am. I'm collecting all these things and bringing them together, and it brings me so much satisfaction and joy."

When I asked her how she would feel if this wasn't a part of her life, her response was quick and her body language obvious. I could see her tense, her face tighten in pain. "When I don't allow for this variation of exposure, I feel like I'm drowning, like I don't have enough oxygen. It makes me crazy. I feel terribly trapped."

And there it was again. Each and every time I ask this question, the response is the same. This is why I share these stories. Brittany and I, we are different in how we approach being women. I worry way too much over it, and she doesn't think about it at all. Our personalities are different, but guess what we share: this crazy inability to show up as ourselves if certain pieces are not being lived out.

Her ferocious curiosity fuels her soul, and what I love about her story is that she finally shook off the persona she felt forced on her, discovered who she was, and is living it. She understands and embraces these pieces in her life that completely and absolutely fuel her soul. She found freedom, joy, and contentment by finally living who she is, and her family, career, and self are healthier and happier because of it. And guess what, she no longer struggles with wondering if she is a "good mom." She knows it.

II

Obstacles

There are a million things that will keep you from feeding your soul. I know because I have many of these in my own life. Some are situational, like my career, some are because I chose to have a family, and some are just plain because I get in the way.

Our circumstances are in large part why we do what we do. Circumstances can exist for long or short seasons. I talk about them because I think it is important to acknowledge what they are and how we use them for our good as well as how they serve as obstacles. Knowing what they are is also imperative to your ability to deal with them in a way that is healthy because we all really want to give our best to everything but that really isn't possible.

Circumstances can flip-flop between forced and chosen. For example, you may choose to work, and there may come a time when you have to work. You may choose a divorce, or your partner may ask for it (one is a chosen circumstance and the other is forced on you). Regardless, they play a role in the obstacles you will face in pursuing your soul care.

Forced Circumstances

Forced circumstances can look like a lot of different things. A forced circumstance can be a job, caring for an ailing parent, helping a family member in a time of need, your own illness or even a divorce or breakup. They are the kind of the things that happen to you, that you don't always choose, or they are an absolute necessity to your existing in the world. Your health is important, as is the health of the people around you, and sometimes you have to step up to either care differently for yourself or others. Your job, well, there isn't any way around that. The bills have to be paid, and let's face it, it's not always how you would want to spend your time. Your job can definitely become an obstacle, and it will surely play a role in the excuses you make around why you will or won't create space to care for yourself. In the research I have done, it is one of the biggest reasons why we don't make the time to care for our souls, and you could argue, it is one of the biggest reasons why we need to.

Chosen Circumstances

Chosen circumstances are sometimes easier to justify because they are things we have chosen, like marriage, family, moving to another city/state, a ministry, charity work, being the room mom at your child's school, etc. They are generally choices about what we want, and yet they consume a good bit of our time. The difference with these obstacles *vs* the ones that are forced is that you sometimes have a love/hate relationship with them.

You want to spend time with your kids. You love date night with your spouse. You are passionate about working with the homeless or the women's ministry at your church. You generally want to do all these things, and yet, when asked, my research showed this was also one of the biggest reasons why women don't make time for themselves.

Remember when I said at the start of this book that women are carriers? We honestly want to do these things. I believe as nurturers we are generally wired to serve, help, carry, and love others. It's why we want to take on all these things. But let's face it, between the forced and the chosen pieces of life, these all become obstacles to our ability to care for ourselves.

You Could Be the Problem

And sometimes, you could be the problem. When you get in your own way, it can sometimes be hard to identify, but if there is anything I have learned, it is that the stories we tell ourselves don't serve us well.

The best way I know how to describe this is by sharing a personal story. When my kids were little, we were living on a limited budget. I was home full time and running my small business out of my home. My hubby was a teacher and coach and worked 12 to 14-hour days, especially during the coaching season. My two kids are 15 months apart, and while I had a lot of experience with children (I'm the old-est of six), I was surprised at how hard it was raising them.

There were a lot of things I didn't understand about myself at the time, like I'm an Enneagram 2 and I refuse to ask for help when I need it. I also am the ENFJ personality type. This type is the least likely of all the "feeling types" to be a stay-at-home parent. Littles are just plain hard, and not all women love being pregnant or having lots of babies (this was my mother. I thought this should be me).

We also didn't have family around, and with my traditional up-bringing I had this notion that I was just supposed to suck it up and never ask for help. Besides, my husband was providing for the family. I needed to keep everything together and under control.

I had a lot of chosen circumstances here, which also meant I had a lot of guilt around being dissatisfied at home. I loved my children, but I had been raised that what I was doing was the calling that had been placed on my life and this meant, sucking it up. This meant I wasn't supposed to question it.

From time to time a girlfriend would ask me to meet for coffee. We would choose a time after the kids went to bed since my hubby was home, and I didn't want to burden him with doing bedtime alone. I would leave, head to the coffee shop, sit down with her, and the whole time I was out I would worry. "What if the kids need me?" "What if my husband gets irritated that I am away?" The next morning if the kids were fussy I'd think, "The kids are super fussy. I should have stayed home last night." If my husband seemed irritable I would think, "Maybe he is mad at me for going out with my friend."

All of these were stories I was making up in my head. I actually created the space to do something for myself, and then I didn't even enjoy it because of the narratives that I was conjuring up. I was getting in the way of my own enjoyment of something I really needed for myself.

Let me give you another, simpler example. Have you ever gotten a massage? You have a full hour on the table and have been looking forward to it for over a week. You lie down, close your eyes, and the whole time you are lying there you are dreading when it will be over because you want to enjoy it. You spend the whole hour hating that it will come to an end. Instead of thoroughly enjoying the time on the table, your mind games steal the enjoyment from the experience. This is a simple example of getting in your own way.

It happens with vacations, the holidays, your birthday, or any special moment. Check yourself and ask how many times you sabotage your own enjoyment either from the untrue stories you are telling yourself or just because you can't be still enough to enjoy it without dreading its end.

But this is the problem: all these things are getting in the way of us taking good care of ourselves, and they are tied (for me) to some deeper issues within my heart and soul.

Selfish Perception

When I feel guilty for taking some time away from my family, what's really going on is I don't want to appear selfish. Women are conditioned in both our wiring and within society that we are to be all things to all people. Think about it: it happens in just about everything we do. I'm always amazed at a man's ability to just say, "I'm not doing that." I'm not going to lie, I usually curse them in my head, but there is a place for boundaries, limits, and the choice not to do some things. Women generally feel this obligation to "pick up all the pieces" or "make the things happen" that men won't do. I can't tell you how many times at work I hear women say, "He just decided he wasn't going to do this piece of his role, so I had to pick up the pieces. I can't let everything fall apart." Who gets to decide they just aren't going to do a part of their job? People can do this because there is usually a woman there trying to fix it and put things back together again.

This can happen at home too. I've seen plenty of guys say, "I'm just not doing that" or "I'm not going to that party" or "I'm not going to chauffer the kids around today." And then what do we do? We huff and puff, roll our eyes, and curse our spouses or partners under our breath. And then we go do it.

We instead need to start asking, do I need to do this? Or if your partner is taking advantage, have a hard conversation about the division of duties. Guess what, ladies? Your partner is just as responsible for things as you are, and sometimes we need to draw lines for ourselves. Sometimes we need to express how much we need help, and sometimes we need to walk away from something that doesn't actually need doing. Taking care of ourselves is not selfish. Taking care of ourselves is necessary in our ability to show up for our families, spouses, friends, and careers.

Approval of Others

I was also too concerned about what people thought about me or about making someone mad or upset. Guess what? Your husband, partner, kids, and even your mom aren't always going to understand, and that is okay. But you can express what you need in a way that helps them understand that you need to take a break so you can be better for yourself and your family.

Lack of Balance

The times when I can't find joy in the moment usually means I haven't done a great job of caring for myself. When I can't even enjoy something I love, this means that I haven't built enough soul care into my regular routine. I dread when my activity is over. Just remember, when you are starving, you generally won't enjoy what you are eating because your most urgent need means you can't take the time to focus on taste. You need nourishment and energy to live. Think about when you enjoy a meal the most—it's when you have been fed, and you have prepared and created the space for the meal. There was probably anticipation about the dining experience, but even if you made the reservation a month prior, you still fed yourself every day before your delicious experience. Feeding your soul is no different. You will sabotage your enjoyment when you fail to refuel yourself in the moments in between.

Finances

Let's face it, money can be a circumstance, obstacle, and even a distraction. Regardless, it is easy to make money an excuse for not feeding your soul. Before I dive into this topic, I first want to acknowledge that money is a true issue for many people. Single parenting, lost jobs, medical bills, and many other factors play into our financial situations. Some are our own doing, and some are based purely on forced circumstances that we never raised our hands for. Lack of funds is a reality, and when it comes between you putting food on the table or paying good money to feed your soul, you are going to put food on the table first.

Personally, I know what this feels like. After I lost my job and my husband was in grad school, we were still living off of a lot more than some folks had, but we were definitely living paycheck to paycheck. Our goal every month was to pay off our credit cards. We lived on a strict budget, but there were months when we wondered if we were going to get by. I remember struggling to buy a tank of gas and couponing to keep our groceries under $100 a week. We didn't have the room in the budget at times for a $4.00 coffee at Starbucks, and a steak dinner was a treat. There was no way during that season that we had the extra cash for passions like painting and sailing, expensive cameras, or even passes to the botanical gardens or museums.

But money isn't needed for everything. When you have less, you have to get scrappy, and sometimes this means getting curious with your limitations. Don't allow your finances to become your excuse. I think it is easy for us in a consumer-driven society to believe that money buys everything. It makes things easier, but it is not necessary to feed your soul.

My challenge to you here is: get curious. It is a great exercise for all of us to do regardless of our financial situations. What do you love to do that costs you nothing or is already a part of your budget that you can capitalize on? It may be singing, sketching with a pencil and paper, hiking all your local parks, or listening to music while you take a bath. It may be writing, blogging, spoken word, working in your yard, or baking a cake for a friend.

Don't allow a lack of money to steal your need for pursuing nourishment for your soul. Practicing this will only help you, and you may just find an even greater sense of gratitude for this season you are currently in.

Fear

I've talked about fear a good bit here. It seems to crop up in a lot of different ways, but ya'll, fear just may be the greatest culprit for why we don't do the things we love. When you don't do something for yourself because you are too concerned about what others will think, that is fear. When you don't want to appear selfish, that is fear. When you sabotage your enjoyment of something, that is rooted in fear. And when you use your finances to tell yourself it's not possible for you, that too is fear.

You are wired to keep yourself safe. You will use fear in almost every area of your life to stay that way. Fear is real. It is crippling. It can stop you in your tracks. It can keep you awake at night. It can torture you in every way possible, and it can keep you from good and beautiful things if you aren't careful.

But let me tell you something, fear is not a reason to keep from pursuing something. It's not a reason to avoid your curiosity. It's not a reason to not go to therapy and get the tools you need to thrive. It's not a reason to keep from questioning the things you were told to become or believe. Fear is not a reason to stop, quit, or stay safe.

Elizabeth Gilbert shares a powerful way she accepted fear in her life in her book *Big Magic*, and her philosophy has transformed the way I interact with fear in my own life. She says, "I don't try to kill off my fear. I don't go to war against it. Instead, I make all that space for it. Heaps of space. Every single day…I allow my fear to live and breathe and stretch out its legs comfortably. It seems to me that the less I fight my fear, the less it fights back. If I can relax, fear relaxes too. In fact, I cordially invite fear to come along with me everywhere I go. I even have a welcoming speech prepared for fear…" (pg. 25).

She goes on to say that when she speaks to fear she says, "I understand you will be joining us [she speaks of creativity as the journey, but you could really insert anything here] because you always do. I acknowledge that you believe you have an important job to do in my life and that you take your job seriously" (pg. 25).

Doesn't this sound about right? Fear on just about any decision to pursue something always seems to show up. Elizabeth says she invites it on the ride. It's there, but she tells fear to take a back seat. She doesn't allow it to drive. She is in the driver's seat with her creative idea by her side and fear in the back. Fear can speak up and it can even caution, but it doesn't get to control.

I find that too many times I'm allowing fear to drive. When I wind up depleted and worn out—at the root of it is fear--fear of failure, fear of not meeting expectations, fear of letting people down, fear of ruining my career. All those fears kept me from taking care of myself because I thought if I did, I would fail. And that just wasn't true.

Recently, I took a new role at work, and after the excitement set in, fear showed up loud and proud. In the learning curve of the new role, I started having thoughts like, "What have I done? Did I make a mistake? Maybe I'm not smart enough for this role." My anxiety was in overdrive. I couldn't sleep. I noticed that fear was not just driving, but taking over everything. I had given it too much space. We had switched seats. I knew all the signs (sleepless nights and the sick feeling in my stomach, racing thoughts that seem to never stop, panic), but guess what really got my attention?

I travel a good bit for work. The winter had been wet, cold, and pretty dreary. I was ready for Spring and desperately needed sunshine. I not only was going crazy with this fear that had completely overcome me, but I came down with something while on the road (which is absolutely miserable).

One of my favorite things about flying is being above the clouds. It can be dark, stormy, and dreary down below, but above the clouds all of that is cleared away. The sky is blue, the sun is bright, and it really is a beautiful, heavenly sight. What is even more amazing is golden hour. Have you ever been on a flight while the sun is setting at 30,000 feet? It is magic.

But on this particular flight home, I looked out the window at 30,000 feet, white fluffy clouds below, the golden skyline ahead of me as the sun set and glistened over the horizon, and I felt nothing. Absolutely nothing. At that moment, I knew I had let fear take over the driver's seat. I was allowing fear to control me.

Something that brings me joy—golden hour above the clouds—is usually a moment that would fuel me and bring me peace, yet I felt empty. I couldn't be nourished because fear was in control. It was a reminder to let fear know that it was time for me to drive.

I'm learning to find gratitude for fear, even make friends with it, because without it I can't be courageous. I can't be curious. I can't foster my needs, and I can't fuel my soul. This concept has changed my perception, and I'm learning more and more to accept that fear will always be there, but it doesn't have to drive. I can.

I share these struggles of mine because, if you are like me, you need to recognize your own self-sabotage. You need to discover what you are doing to keep yourself from nourishment. You need to get curious and ask why. And you need to discover tactics to help you circumvent what you, most likely, will naturally do. It is the first step to moving into a place where you can give yourself permission to feed your soul.

"I had started signing up for everything... It was becoming too much, and I realized, I've got to simplify things at home. These things were stressing me, not bringing me joy and I knew I wasn't showing up well to my kids, husband, or at work."

Laura

Interlude

Laura's Story

My friend Laura is a fun, vivacious person. You can always count on Laura to jump up and dance to any song that begets "get up and move." She's funny, smart, and one of those folks you can count on getting real; she's not the kind of person to b.s. you.

She sought me out, really wanting to discuss this topic after I made the shameless plug on my Facebook feed. I was interested to hear what she had to say. As I explained the project to her and what I was really looking for out of the interview, I could see her wheels turning. Laura should never play poker. You can read her like an open book, and it's something I love about her.

She started by asking a question, "Do you want me to get real?" Of course, I agreed and she obliged.

Laura started her story at a point several years ago. She's a wife, mother of two cuties, and an executive administrator. She had just been handed supporting two busy and impactful leaders and their teams, and she was struggling to handle it all. Her kids were little, and she felt like things were out of control. She came to a breaking point, finally raising her hand and saying to her bosses, "I can't do this."

"That was really hard for me," she said to me. "Having to admit that I couldn't handle the workload was not only humbling, but I felt like something was wrong with me. Thankfully, the leaders I was working for heard me and shifted the work so I was only serving one of them. It was hard because I cared about both of them and the work, and I wanted to do it all. But I had to admit to myself that something had to give."

She also realized that something had to give at home, too. "I had started signing up for everything--serving at my kids' school, serving in the neighborhood, church, and the kids activities started ramping up. It was becoming too much, and I realized I would have to simplify things at home. These things were stressing me, not bringing me joy, and I knew I wasn't showing up well to my kids, husband, or work."

Laura also decided to implement a daily quiet time into her routine focused on prayer, reading, and journaling. "It was like a breath of fresh air, and I immediately felt a difference when I did it. If I skipped, I could tell throughout my day. It made a difference." She also started incorporating daily exercise. "I was in the best shape of my life," she said.

"I was in a steady routine of self-care; things were clicking along. Fast forward to 2019, and I have no idea why I did it, but I started letting things creep back in. I started signing up for things at school—I became my son's room mom and started serving on my neighborhood board." Then 2019 wound up being one of the hardest years of her life at work, and she became completely overwhelmed.

Last year she started having some health problems. Bouts of

dizziness were keeping her out of commission. After a particularly rough time, she went to the doctor. They treated her for a viral infection that they said was affecting her inner ear, and she got better. Six months later, it was back again, and this time, the same approach didn't work. The dizziness continued. Doctors struggled to diagnose her. They couldn't find a source, and her anxiety started spiraling. She insisted on getting an MRI. She was thinking the worst.

"I kind of get something stuck in my head, and I won't let it go until I know it's not a possibility. I have to rule it out to rest. And I was taking this to the extreme—a brain tumor. What else could it be? I kept thinking about my kids and my husband, and I let myself worry and fret over a life that my kids would live without their mother." The doctor was sure it was nothing of the kind. The MRI was not ordered, and her fears continued.

She knew she was taking it too far, but it was like she couldn't help herself. She said, "I know it sounds crazy. I mean, when I say it out loud, it is crazy." But I'm curious, how many of us have taken a narrative and blown it out of proportion. I know I certainly have.

She said her husband was a trooper through the whole thing, but he was getting tired of her irrational behavior. She said, "I knew I was being ridiculous, but I just couldn't make myself believe that there wasn't something seriously wrong with me. They had to have missed something." Everything came to a head the night she came home from a cruise. She had taken the patch for nausea while on board, and the day she switched patches her eyes went completely blurry. "It tipped me over the edge."

By the time she got off the ship and was headed home, her dizziness was out of control. Her mom had the kids, and her husband insisted on taking her to the emergency room. They ran tests, checked her out, and still nothing. But the doctor was clear. He was confident he knew what was going on. You guessed it; she nearly had a full-blown panic attack. The dizziness, he concluded, was also stress-related, and the vision issues were related to the patch she used on the boat.

She told me she started seeing a therapist for the first time in her life after that night, and they put her on anti-anxiety meds. Guess what, not one dizzy spell! I could tell she was disappointed in herself. "I knew. I knew that I had let life creep. I had taken on too much, and it all caught up to me." It was time to cut back—she put some boundaries back into her life, let go of some of her responsibilities outside of work, continued with therapy, and is doing her daily quiet time.

I asked her how these things make her feel and what happens when she isn't doing them. She said, "I'm not sure I know what activities feed my soul. I'm not sure I've discovered what you have described. But I can feel it when I don't do them. Things feel off. My day doesn't go as well, and I know it makes a difference."

Laura and I talked for a few minutes about the void of soul care in her life. I could see her pondering it, asking herself, "What could it be?" And while she wasn't sure she had fully discovered it, she knew she needed it, even if it was practicing the things she had learned in her experiences over the last several years. "I'm in a reset season--working with a therapist, managing stress and anxiety—I'm taking it one step at a time, and I'm looking forward to what may come out of it." And I know she is.

I share Laura's story because I'm guessing in some way, you have lived her story. Many of us get to these places where we are spiraling. We've loaded our plates way too high with too many things we are doing for others. We are feeding everyone else, and then if we fix a plate for ourselves it is so small, we barely get anything to eat.

Laura's story is just another example of how obstacles can get in our way and fear can take control. The stories we tell ourselves can be damaging if we take them too far. We all need to care for our souls.

You may have no idea where you are in your journey right now and like Laura, have zero idea of whether or not you have found what feeds your soul. But my friend, this doesn't mean you can't start somewhere. Start with the tools you find here. Heck, do what Laura did. She decided to find a book to read, set the timer (even if it was for 8 minutes), and let herself have that time to enjoy every page of her book.

This discovery may be a journey for you and may take some time, and that is okay. But I beg you, do something because every little step you take towards it is only going to help you become the best version of yourself. You (and everyone else) need that version of you—not the strung out, I think I'm going to die, stressed-out version. That person isn't you. That person is not at the core of who you are. That person is covering up the beautiful spirit that is intended for this world. And that person is never going to allow you to live a life that is full and meaningful.

12

Setting Expectations for Yourself and Others

You may be asking, how do I discover what my obstacles are and how might I be getting in my own way? How do I create tactics to help circumvent what I will use as excuses in my life? This is another one of those things that is different for everyone.

Self-reflection takes a little bit of time. It doesn't have to take a ton, but we are busy in our lives. We sometimes don't allow ourselves to understand fully what is swirling around us. We are just swirling with it.

But the "how" can sometimes look like taking 30 minutes to an hour one morning or evening, waking early or forgoing a Netflix show, grabbing a pen and paper—or better yet, just have a beautiful journal and your favorite pen ready to go. Take a few deep breaths and start writing. Write how you feel. Write down the load of things you have on your plate. Write down your forced and chosen circumstances. Write down your excuses: money, time, and the other things you know are getting in your way. Write until you don't think you have anything left. Just empty yourself on that piece of paper and then stop. Sometimes I like to walk away from it for a day or two and let it settle there on the pages. I call this a brain or soul dump exercise, and it is when I come back to it and reread it that I can start making more sense out of it.

When you come back to it, start highlighting or circling the key pieces—the ones you feel certain are getting in your way. It will help you create an inventory or list for the next exercise we will discuss in a few pages.

Hopefully doing this exercise will give you better clarity on what is going on in your life. You may be surprised at what emerges. I also think it is important to acknowledge what you can own and get control of.

Your next step is to take this list and use it to understand and accept your energy levels, as well as really evaluate the things you are involved in. It's an important step to building boundaries so you can create more time for things that fuel your soul.

First, it is important to realize we all have different energy levels. Our seasons of life will determine this, but your age and interests will as well. Some of you enjoy having a full calendar. You don't like to sit. You are on the go and like to have all the whitespace on your calendar filled.

Others of you prefer time at home, need a lot of alone time to recharge, and basically prefer your PJs *vs* showing your face. You would create even more whitespace on the calendar if you could.

And then there are a lot of us in the middle. None of these scenarios is bad. We all just have different types of capacity and energy levels.

And this is what this looks like for me. I place myself somewhere in the middle on energy level and need for activity. I know this about myself now. I can start evaluating what is on my plate and if my energy level is a match. If you know you are in good balance, you may want to skip this step. If it is off kilter, it's time to take that brain dump and start creating categories like work, home, kids, etc. Once these items are categorized, it's a good practice to go through each item and ask, does this energize or drain me? You may have an entire bucket that falls into only one of those descriptors. This is a good indication that you may need to evaluate a few things. Please don't hear me say that if it doesn't energize, you don't do it. That isn't feasible, but it will help you understand where you may need to ask for help, take a break, or even consider where to scale back.

Here is how I have broken this down and assessed this for myself. My reality is I have two kids, a career, and a hubby who works. I travel a lot for work, and my kids are at ages where they are involved in a lot and need us to get them to and from everything. We have a couple of rules for our sanity, and so I actually can create time for myself. The kids are allowed ONE extracurricular activity outside of school and ONE in school—not three, not five. ONE.

Our reasoning is that time outside of work and school hours is limited, and being available for those activities, plus driving to and from, results in a lot of time commitment and a lot of energy drain. I have learned that too many extracurriculars really add to my stress level. They drain me. Because of this, we also forgo activities in the summer (outside of camps). My kids haven't participated in sports or activities that require summer involvement. That works for us. I'm a big believer in taking a season off once a year. Everyone needs a little down time, and you may be surprised at what other things you can incorporate—one being a novel idea: rest.

I also am very selective about what I involve myself in. For instance, I do little volunteering at my kids' school. I felt guilty about this for years, but here is the thing: I don't enjoy it. It drains my energy, and I would rather spend the time with my children at home *vs* with most of their classmates for an hour during the week.

There are seasons when I don't volunteer for anything, but when I do, I am intentional about it because my time is valuable. I choose something I am passionate about, again leaning into what gives me energy *vs* what drains me. I struggled with guilt over these decisions in the past, but when I choose to volunteer out of obligation, I find myself frustrated and resentful.

When this happens (because it still does), I have to remind myself that some things don't need to be done, and a lot of things don't need me in the equation. Remember, we can't be everything to everyone—especially when we aren't doing a great job of taking care of ourselves. When tasks are leaving us worse off than when we started, I ask, is this job really intended for me to do, or am I feeling obligated to do it? If it's the latter, I generally strike it from the list.

I also think it is important to note that you may need an extreme slashing of the schedule and paring down at the start. You may need to step out of all your extra activities for a while until you can accomplish better balance. This may seem crazy, but practicing balance and learning to incorporate this practice of nourishing your soul takes space and repetition. Once you get your sea legs and build your confidence around your practices, you will be better able to step out again and help.

You may believe this sounds selfish, but this is part of the problem. Our overscheduling of ourselves and our families is a huge issue. We don't value rest, and if you are feeling stuck, overwhelmed, and like something needs to give, something probably does. You are the only person who can start to put this into motion, and you are the only one who knows just how much energy you need to be in a good, healthy place.

When you take this inventory, evaluate your energy levels and ask yourself, what actually can give? What should I stop doing? Ask yourself, am I really giving my time to things intentionally, or am I giving of myself to others outside of my immediate family out of pure obligation? Let me be the first to tell you, this isn't worth it. Your chosen circumstances are just that--of your choosing. Start some intentional and prioritized selection.

If you took advantage of these exercises I have suggested and started your prioritization, here is a next step. Take what's left—those things that just have to stay or the ones that you chose because they don't drain you—and start asking some specific questions. It will help you refine your list even more. Ask:

1. Is this serving me well or am I doing this out of obligation? (I find this as an easy indicator of one or two things to strike.)
2. What do I enjoy?
3. What do I not enjoy?
4. What do my kids enjoy?
5. What does my partner enjoy and what does he or she hate?
6. What do we all have to prioritize?

Once you get through your own self-evaluation and have a pretty solid list, it's time to involve the kids or your partner. If you are single, I recommend talking with your closest friend or a family member who knows you well and ask them to evaluate your list. Tell them what you are trying to accomplish; and just state, given what you know about me, what should I consider striking from this list? With my kids, I ask them to rate their top one or two activities. I get my husband to do the same. This helps you understand what is more important to them, which also may come as a surprise; they may not be that interested in a few activities and are just doing them out of obligation or because it was offered. If you want to take this a step further, involve your partner and get them to go through the same exercise. Work together to set a goal for how much time you want to free up, and understand if there are areas for which you would like to incorporate more together time as a family or even with each other. It's really wonderful to have everyone on the same page with the plan.

Whether you have discovered what nourishes you or not, this exercise will help you be able to create the space to practice it or the space to continue your journey of discovering it. The great thing about doing this with your partner is it allows you to have honest conversations about what you are going to continue to do and how you each will or won't be involved. If you are on your own, then use that accountability partner I mentioned. I think it's easy to allow the creep of life (unless you are disciplined) to happen, and this exercise can bring all those balls you are juggling back into some kind of alignment.

In a coupled or family situation, talking these things out and creating that plan is really important to your success. I remember when my kids were in first and second grade. I had just gone back to work, and I was feeling overwhelmed. I felt like I was going to cave with all the responsibilities; and then one day I realized these little people that live with me can wipe down the counters after lunch, unload most of the dishwasher, and learn to fold and put away their clothes. And just like that, my kids became more responsible, and I freed up a little more time on my plate. It was a gamechanger.

My husband and I also had to talk through some division of duties. He was accustomed to me doing most of the housework, shopping, doctor's appointments, and cooking. I was also responsible for getting the kids to and from school. We wound up hiring a housekeeper to help with housework, he started taking the kids to school, and we shared the responsibility of taking the kids to the doctor.

I am also not against paying other people to do things. I have not always been able to afford this and realize that any time you can afford to pay someone to clean your house, run your errands, or iron your clothes, it is a luxury. But ladies, if you can afford it and still have a healthy budget, then do it. If having your house cleaned for you means that you can spend your Saturday morning going to breakfast with your kids, attending a yoga class, or painting in your studio, then by all means, the money spent is worth every cent.

Now that you have a plan, you have prioritized what you feel is important, and you have found space to foster and nourish what fuels your soul. You may start feeling a little bit more like you are gaining control—and that is good—but I think it's important that we talk about one area you can't control: other people's expectations.

Sigh… this one is probably the hardest one for me. I love my kids, my husband, and my mom, but their needs and expectations can't and shouldn't always be met in the way they want them met. Please don't get me wrong, relationships are a two-way street, but if you are starving and in desperate need of nourishment for your soul, your people may not fully understand, especially if you have been taking care of them instead of occasionally taking care of yourself. Let's explore how you can address the expectations with each of the important people in your life.

Your Kids

Your kids are not going to understand why you need to take an afternoon hike without them. Your decision to fuel your soul will not register with them. They may cry. They may whine. They may even resent you, but it is important for kids to realize that your world does not always revolve around them. Your life, needs, wants, and desires exist outside of being a mom. You have interests, passions, and pursuits that are outside of motherhood, and that is perfectly okay. Not only is it okay, it is healthy. Your kids need to see that their lives don't need to revolve around only you. Your kids need to see an example of healthy balance and good self-care. And your kids need the best version of their mother.

Your care of yourself doesn't mean that you don't love your kids. It is important for you to weigh the cost. When you choose to forgo what you need and not take a break to refuel, what happens? You may be feeling guilty about taking the time to refuel, but how guilty do you feel when you are screaming at your kids and can't wait to get them in bed just so you can grab some time for yourself? You can't be present with your kids and love them well if you aren't taking time to feed your soul.

Your Partner

This goes for our spouses or partners too. This one is hard for me. My husband and I love to do things together, but we also have very different passions. It is important that we support each other in our need to do things that we love outside of our relationship. And it is important to ask for what we need. This is hard for many of us to do. I don't want to "inconvenience" my husband, but if he had half a clue that I was about to blow my gasket due to my stress levels, I promise you he would be ushering me out the door. He knows as well as I do that if I create this space for myself, I'll be better at home and with him.

Your Other Family and Friends

Now, I love my friends and extended family, but this is another area where you need boundaries. All these people mean well, but you may be doing too much, and you (and they) may not even realize it.

I've mentioned before that women are carriers, and if I know something about women, we do a whole lot of stuff for a lot of people out of sheer obligation--not because we want to, not because we need to, but because we feel like we are expected to, and we don't want to upset the people around us.

But let me remind you again—you can't be everything to everyone. You will never make everyone happy. Setting a boundary doesn't mean that you don't care about the people in your life, and if they revolt even after you have told them why you need to prioritize feeding your soul, then they are only concerned with what they are getting out of the relationship. Yes, even family—your parents, siblings, etc.—may unintentionally be more concerned with what they are getting out of your relationship than with you taking care of yourself. This is hard stuff, and feelings may be hurt, but if this is an issue for you, I encourage to read *Boundaries* by Dr. Henry Cloud and Dr. John Townsend. Additionally, if you are like me, you may also need a therapist to walk through this with you. Creating boundaries and honoring relationships takes time and work, and people won't always understand. Talking with your therapist about how to make it happen may be just what you need.

Your Career

Let's not forget about our careers because in my survey I found for many women this is the one thing outside of their families that takes the majority of their time. Let's face it, many companies are not really concerned about your self-care practices, but they are really interested in you getting the job done. There is no way you can do a good job without sacrificing something somewhere, and what do you usually sacrifice? The one thing that is going to sustain you in all the obstacles you face every day. You can make a lot of personal excuses, and even bring up the obstacles we talked about before to keep you from doing the one thing that is going to help you be a better wife, mom, and employee.

I share this because, like me, you need to recognize it. It is the first step to moving into a place where you can give yourself permission to feed your soul. Don't let your career be an obstacle and start putting some boundaries into place.

You may be wondering, how do you put boundaries up at work? It's a good question because sometimes putting up a boundary can mean losing your job. Before we go there, I'll tell you about a simple one I put into practice recently, and then we will venture down that scary road.

My super simple boundary was this: I turned my email notifications off on my phone. This means, I will go all day without seeing that number continually rise as I sit through meeting after meeting. At first, I wasn't sure. I thought, I'll try this for a couple of weeks and see. My goal is responsiveness, and I generally want to make sure I'm addressing needs as they come in. I had also tricked myself into thinking that doing this made me more productive. What's funny is I haven't missed a beat, and I'm amazed at how much less stress I feel by not seeing those email notifications on my phone.

I still believe in being responsive, but now I set designated time aside to address emails at the start and end of each day. This one simple boundary played a huge role in helping me feel less chaotic and has freed up my mind space creating more presence with the people I love.

But for the bigger stuff, I want to challenge you with this. If you are not with a company or have a boss to whom you can go to share your struggles, I am sorry. I know this can be the norm more often than not. But a lot of times you have to start somewhere. Let me tell you about one thing I did when I went back to work.

We were not a remote working environment, and I did not have enough seniority to have the autonomy to handle work schedules like I would want to. I wanted to have at least one remote day occasionally so I could focus on development and go to lunch with my kids. I created a plan. Not wanting to be too greedy or presumptuous, I went to my boss and asked him for one remote day a quarter. I explained what I wanted to do and clearly outlined my desire to take time during that day to have lunch with my kids at school. You know what he said? He told me he wanted me to do this at least once a month. I was floored. I felt heard, appreciated, and I totally took him up on it.

Y'all, I wasn't asking my employer to give me a day to go explore and practice my soul care. I was asking them for a remote day when I could get really focused on work and have lunch with my kids because it was meaningful to all of us. That adjustment gave me more time to get my work done. This meant I felt less stress, was working less at night, and was still able to love on my kiddos in a way they were used to (which meant I wasn't looking for this after hours). It benefited me greatly, and it freed up space.

Now here is the hard part. A helpful response is not always the outcome; and if you find your employer won't budge, it may be time to start asking yourself some hard questions about what you do, what you can change, and if this is the right environment for you. Yes, you may have to compromise. Yes, you may have to have a respectful conversation with your boss and ask for help. And yes, you may have to make a plan to eventually leave (if that is what you discover you need).

These are not easy decisions, but I'm going to guess that at the end of your life you won't be remembering and reliving the nights and days you spent slaving away over your career. You will be wishing you had figured out how to make more time for the things that were important in your life.

Avoiding Comparison

How many times have you heard the quote, "Comparison is the thief of joy?" I've heard it so many times that I fail to ponder it anymore, but it's true. We women are really good at comparing ourselves.

You may be thinking, "Oh, I'm really not that bad. I'm not comparing myself to her." But how many times are we comparing our clothes, circumstances, choices we have made for our children, our religion, what we drive, and more? And let's think about our bodies. I have not met one single woman that doesn't compare her appearance to another woman or women. NOT ONE! Even the most beautiful women I know compare themselves to the ideal standard of perfection they have in their mind. We all do it, and comparison is something you will have to guard against when it comes to feeding your soul.

I have a lot of women tell me all the time, "Oh, Alison, I'm not nearly as creative as you are," or "I wish I knew how to do that, but I don't have a creative bone in my body." I know I've done it with others. Sometimes I wish my soul care involved some sort of exercise because if I was passionate about it and it didn't feel like such a chore, I'd do it all the time (and I'd have the results to go with it; and that is even comparison).

I hope that when you discover what feeds your soul, you choose to see it as the gift that it is. I hope you don't look around and say, "Man, I wish mine looked like hers," or get some kind of complex, thinking that you are uninteresting or weird or over the top. The beautiful thing about your feeding your soul is that it is completely unique to you. And if you get joy and pleasure from something and it is straight up making you a better person, then relish in the gift and don't get caught up in comparing what you like *vs* what others have. Comparison is definitely not the point of soul care, and it will be a thief of your joy!

Now that you have identified the things that take your time, considered what gives you energy and what doesn't, and determined priorities, take some time to complete a few journal entries about what expectations could get in your way. I'd also rank them on which one you believe would be the hardest to tackle.

I've created an activity for you on the next page to use if you like. It allows you to take all that journaling and listing and put it onto one page so that you can see and identify your priority map. There is something a little freeing about this exercise when you are done.

setting expectations for yourself and others

You can feel the stress roll off as you say "no" to nonessentials and get to say "yes" to more things you and your family enjoy. Make sure if you have identified what feeds your soul that it makes the "yes" list.

activity

Priority List Worksheet

In the hustle and bustle of life, everything can seem like it needs to be a priority. But if you are trying to create margin in your life, not everything can be. This exercise is simply a way for you to identify what you actually have going on, determine what you need to prioritize, and maybe even eliminate the non-necessary activities to create margin.

Directions:

List everything you have going on in the first section. Think about which activities are essential and which are not. In the second section, pull out the activities that are essential and then list non-essential in the third section. Once complete, really evaluate what is essential and what isn't. Could more items land in the non-essential category if you take into account the information we just discussed? Remember, 3-5 priorities for your family is probably healthy. Try to create your new list with that in mind.

List all activities

_____

_____

_____

_____

List all essential activities

As an additional step feel free to mark what drains you and what energizes you on the list above. You can repeat this on your list of non-essential activities. Place an "x" for draining and "o" for energizing.

List all non-essential activities

_____

_____

_____

_____

_____

_____

_____

_____

_____

_____

_____

Now, what is your new list?

_____

_____

_____

_____

_____

_____

_____

_____

_____

_____

The full worksheet is available in my workbook on www.alisonenglish.com/resources.

section 5

Application

13

Give Yourself Permission

When you start learning to put boundaries in place, you will be amazed at how free you feel in your life. Remember, you can never be all things to all people, and you certainly can't take care of yourself if this is your mentality. If you are new to it, learning to set expectations for yourself and others is going to take practice. The more you do it, the more confident you will become and the more your people will start to understand. Those that love you will also see the change in you, and they will cheer you on.

You may be asking, what does application actually look like? I think it is different for every person. I would say I was an extreme case, and setting expectations for myself and others is still a battle. As a chronic people-pleaser with high anxiety, I believe there is an element of this I will most likely battle all my life. For me, it is about taking baby steps.

The first place to start is to give yourself permission. This next little tactic is one I used to help me get over the hump. It's how I gave myself permission to do what I loved. This is all about your writing your own statement and believing it, but I've given you an example to get you started:

"I give myself permission to fuel my soul through _____. The purpose of this time is to practice _____, open my heart to regular inspiration, enjoy _____ and withhold judgment on what unfolds here. This time is intended for me. This activity serves as a way to nourish my soul—not please others, not foster praise for a job well done. The act of _____ is to spark joy and gratitude and to feed my soul."

Once you have your statement written, I suggest you keep it in your journal or use it as a bookmark in that development book you are reading. Keep it close enough that if you start feeling that you just can't grant yourself permission to care for your soul, it's there to remind you that you can.

If you don't feel like you need therapy after reading about dealing with circumstances and setting expectations, congratulations. That whole chapter is probably worth about ten years of my own soul searching, counseling, reading, and prayer and a lot of work on self (which quite frankly is not finished). The beautiful thing is you have the ability to make this happen for yourself. It's time to do some work and put things into practice, and if you need therapy, well that is okay, too.

14

Putting Soul Care into Practice

If you have made it this far, I hope you are not feeling overwhelmed, but rather are experiencing a sense of accomplishment. You have worked through a lot, and my hope is that you are at least pondering what soul care could look like for you, as well as starting to understand how you can make it happen and the obstacles you might face.

If you have a few activities that you have identified for your soul care practice, you may be wondering how to implement them. This will be different for many of you, but through my experience and talking with others, this next section will provide a few ways for you to start thinking about how to incorporate and plan what fuels you, developing practices that you can use regularly.

Warning Before You Start

I do want to give you a little warning before you start. Personally, when I think of the word "practice," I generally do not have positive feelings. It reminds me of piano lessons, setting the timer and slaving away every afternoon over pieces that I rarely enjoyed. Or it brings back the spiritual disciplines I learned growing up in my Christian faith: the seven steps to an effective prayer life, the three steps to Scripture reading, or five ways to worship. This may fuel you, but for me, it's a drag! Seriously, if it gets too meticulous, it loses its fun or mystery. When you discover something that fuels your soul like I did in painting and creativity, and you determine to set up a regular practice, I want to warn you about making it too structured.

We will talk a bit more about this when we get to the scheduling activity coming up, but first I want to go into some key ingredients that I believe can help quiet the ego, enlivening the soul--preparing it for the activities you are cultivating to fuel it. You don't have to do all of them, or you can do them in conjunction with one another. Remember, these are suggestions. You pick and choose what works for you, but I encourage you at least to get curious about each one of them and give them a try. I find the more I incorporate them, the better I am—I'm more open to what creativity brings my soul, my ego is quieter, and I'm definitely more in tune in my relationship with God.

Preparing Yourself to Feed Your Soul

As we move into talking through these important ingredients, remember at the start when we began talking about how the ego is usually driving and the soul is ignored? These ingredients, when done with intention, will help you to quiet the ego so you can tune into the soul.

I believe these practices can help cultivate and prepare your soul to receive what nourishes it. Not to get too technical about what each of these things mean, I want to offer some simple sentiment about each one. You can take or leave how and if these ingredients will help you foster a meaningful practice. And, again, these serve as my ingredients to fostering soul care, but they could very well serve as a way to feed your soul too.

Creating Atmosphere

When was the last time your breath was taken away purely by the atmosphere you were in? It could have been in nature, in an art gallery, or in an airplane looking across the vast expanse of sky. It could have been at a new restaurant, your favorite coffee shop, or a boutique. Positively or negatively, we all resonate with atmosphere.

I love this definition of atmosphere from *dictionary.com*: "the pervading tone or mood of a place, situation, or work of art." A tone or mood that permeates everything surrounding you can fuel you if you let it. Just think about it, a wedding without atmosphere doesn't feel as celebratory. A movie without atmosphere could feel strange or fall flat. A candlelit dinner with soft music can make a date more romantic, and creating an attractive, positive atmosphere for activities you love can elevate the experience to an entirely new level.

I've also found that creating atmosphere even in everyday activities can elevate the experience. For example, every morning I basically have the same routine. I wash my face, moisturize, put on my make-up, and fix my hair. This generally takes me 30 to 45 minutes, depending on how I style my hair. It's a good bit of time, and there are days I dread it, wishing I didn't care as much about my appearance.

When I started to understand the need for soul care in my life, I discovered this lovely little trick. In that 30 to 45 minutes, I create an atmosphere that is beautiful and relaxing and brings me joy. A simple candle and my favorite playlist, and I've transformed a dreaded daily chore into something that I not only enjoy, it brings me a good bit of satisfaction. I've fueled my soul.

I've found the trick works for a good many things. It accentuates that time when I paint. Cooking dinner feels more like a special moment, and even over the holidays I created an atmosphere while I hand-addressed 100 Christmas cards. Something that usually felt like such a chore wound up being a lovely way to enjoy an evening, and I walked away feeling refreshed. Never underestimate the power of how an atmosphere can make you feel.

Solitude

Solitude for some may be something that you absolutely relish. You never need an excuse to steal away. Others may be petrified to think about spending too much time in solitude, and if you are like me in my younger years, I tried my best to avoid it. I find when you are single, childless, or an empty nester, solitude is something you have in spades. You may not even think about it because quite frankly, you've got plenty. But how are you using that solitude?

I recently met with two friends completely independent of one another. Both single women of different races, completely different careers, and a gap in age of around a dozen years, and both admitted their avoidance of solitude. When I pressed them as to why, it was almost as if they had too much. They admitted needing it to practice self-care but would still avoid it, even if it meant they didn't get to do something they enjoyed. I get it. If you are alone all the time, why would you want more alone time?

If you are a young mother or busy with a career, or even caring for a sick loved one and are on call 24/7, you may feel that solitude is impossible. You may want it desperately, but there is no time to yourself. It's just not going to happen. Yet it is an important ingredient to fostering your soul care and quieting the ego.

Solitude is the state of being alone. Have you ever sat alone with your ego? Have you ever sat alone with your soul? These are interesting questions, but they are good ones. You will need solitude to quiet the ego so that you aren't distracted by comparison or success, the fear of failure, or not feeling good enough. Being alone is necessary to answer these questions. It is imperative to listening to what you observe about your ego and what you hear from your soul. Solitude is a must.

Quiet

Quiet might seem like a given since I've now insisted that you get some time alone. Remember, you can control the parameters of what each of these ingredients looks like. The time you need to spend on each element will vary with your need.

Quiet is also relative. What do I mean by this? Before I had kids, if I was quiet and alone, I would turn on music or even the TV just to have some sound. It wasn't distracting or loud. The music was particularly stimulating and enhanced the "quiet" of that time. After I had both of my kids, I remember sitting in my living room while they both napped and completely reveled in absolute silence. I sat there for an hour without a peep of noise, and it was amazing.

Now, for me, quiet usually looks like soft tunes, generally instrumental. I've moved back to a place where it energizes the quiet space. Only you can know what quiet means for you and what you need, but it is a natural complement to solitude. Besides, you can't listen to your soul if there is too much noise. The point is to diminish distractions–physical and mental.

Breathing

This brings us to breathing. Ah, those mental distractions. I've long taken the natural state and pattern of breathing for granted. Science teaches us the vital importance of our breath, but it has cleansing and calming properties as well. I recently took a breathwork class, and I've never felt so clear and in tune. It wiped many of the mental cobwebs clean.

If that is too intense for you, the simple act of noticing your breath can not only calm, but also focus the mind. Simply breathing in deeply, then out, or even counting the breaths can bring you more focus. Remember, the goal is to see, to hear, and to give your soul a chance to speak. This is hard to do when your mind is racing with a million things. Focusing on the breath helps to quiet the mind enabling you to check in.

I do find this can be hard for people when they have never done it before. If this is you, set your timer for 3 to 5 minutes, close your eyes and breathe in and out. You can count each breath to ten and start over. Try to breathe normally. Your only focus during that time is on the breath.

If you find that doesn't work, there are other apps and resources online that can help. When I first started, several apps really helped. I used *Mindspace* for a year and still use *Centering Prayer* to walk me through the process on occasion (these can be found in your app store, and both have free options). I also enjoy looking for guided meditations online (*YouTube* has quite a few). There are a lot of free options, and some may be perfect for you. Some of my personal favorites are from *The Honest Guys* and *The Mindfulness Movement*.

Look at these options as a practice round, and once you figure out your preferences, you can use breathing on a regular basis for self-check-ins (it also works great for reducing stress, too).

Another thing I like about taking a few minutes to tune into your breathing is that it puts you in the present. Your mind may wander, but every time you come back to your breath, you are sitting with yourself in the "now." It's always interesting to me to notice just how distracted I am and how rarely I am actually in the present. I'm usually running through a laundry list, stressing over something in the future, feeling bad about something in the past, thinking about lunch, irritated, or my favorite, stuck in a spiral about body image. When I stop to focus on my breath, it helps me pay attention to the present.

This practice also generally conjures up gratitude. Why? Because when you notice your breath, you notice the gift of life. I typically never think about breathing because I do it automatically. When I notice my breath, I am reminded of the life I have been given in this moment, and I have gratitude for the gift of breath that continues to fill my body with life.

Meditation

Depending on your faith or beliefs, meditation can take on a lot of different forms. Meditation is part of my prayer life, but it is taking solitude, quiet, and breath and bringing them all together. It is generally in meditation that I both quiet the ego but also make my personal connections to God. It is what I believe God intended when he told us in Scripture to "Be still and know that I am God." What's strange is I'm not talking to Him in these times. I'm not praying. I'm being still, alone and quiet, using my breath to focus and ground me.

You may find yourself quoting a Scripture, reciting a mantra, or using a word of intention to make the meditation even more meaningful. Meditation is broader than any set ritual. This practice can help you reconnect with your soul.

Nature

"And into the forest I go to lose my mind and find my soul."

John Muir

In nearly every conversation I had with the women I interviewed for this book, nature came up. I realize there are a few of you that wouldn't call yourself the "nature" type, but many of us feel a stirring, quiet, spiritual connection when we are in and experiencing nature.

My favorite place is by the ocean. I've long told my loved ones that when I die, I want my ashes spread there. My soul finds peace by the ocean, dusk or golden hour being my absolute favorite. Sitting there until the sun sets for me it is the closest thing to heaven on earth and nourishes my soul ten-fold.

I have also found this power in the beauty of the Rocky Mountains, the valleys of Appalachia, the rolling, green hills of Kentucky and the forests of my home state of Georgia. Regardless of your belief system, it really should come as no surprise that the natural world around us feels connected to our beings. It's the one thing that my non-Christian friends and family and I can agree on: there is something spiritual about experiencing nature. Nature not only prepares and clears my mind so that I can "hear" from my soul and quiet my ego, it also fuels me.

Journaling

I find journaling helps me to get the crap out. Most of the time when I can't quiet my mind and there is something on repeat, writing it out by journaling about it helps to get it out. I find that sometimes I also find answers there—like what is really going on with my feelings or answers to things that are stressing me out.

I generally feel that God meets me in that activity as well because as I journal, I sense that He helps bring those answers. It also helps me identify where my ego is showing up, and it allows me to identify the questions I need to ask myself to get back to my soul.

I've also found that journaling fosters my creativity. I don't think it is a coincidence that "morning pages," as Julia Cameron calls them in her book *The Artist's Way*, are a key piece of her instructions to rid an artist of creative block. Most of our own crap is what is getting in our way (and it is generally centered in the ego). Journaling has a way of cutting through what some of these other practices sometimes can't accomplish. The act of emptying myself on a page allows me to relieve my mind and soul of the burdens I'm carrying.

activity

Soul Care Recipe

The purpose of this recipe is for you to take all or some of the elements discussed in this chapter and prepare your soul for care. These can be done before the activity you have decided to pursue or as part of your daily or weekly routine. The intent is to quiet the ego so that you can experience your soul in a dynamic way.

Review the card on the next page as a starting point and take a few minutes to define what each of these topics mean for you. If these aren't part of your recipe, use the blank card (provided on pg.148) to make your own list.

Once you have created your list, on the back of your card write your intention for this activity. Example: "I commit to practicing these activities on a daily basis to help foster soul care in my life." or "This recipe card serves as a reminder to incorporate these activities to foster soul care in my daily life."

Keep the card in your journal, devotional, or by your bed as a reminder. As your journey progresses, these attitudes and intentions may grow.

Example of what I have on my recipe card and how I use it:

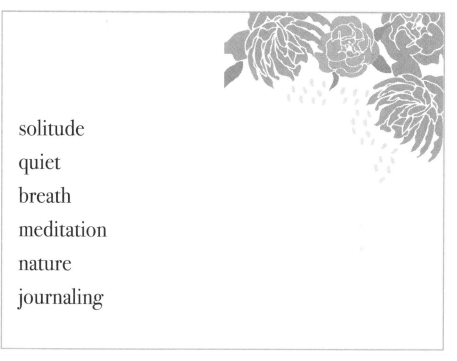

solitude

quiet

breath

meditation

nature

journaling

I personally use this card as a reminder-primarily to help me evaluate what I know works for me. This helps me during times where I tend to let these activities slide. I can ask, "how have I been incorporating these things lately?" If the answer is "not much," then I ask myself what I want to start incorporating in my routine.

This is just one way to use this card. Feel free to explore other creative ways to use this card as you move through your soul care journey.

my soul care recipe

-
-
-
-
-
-

Here is blank card for your use, or download a more scalable card from my website at alisonenglish.com/resources.

15

Planning Time to Feed Your Soul

Now that we have talked through several ingredients for fostering what feeds your soul, let's get into some more practical tips. These tips are more specific to the activities you like to do and will be more tailored to you.

If you chose to do any of the worksheets prior to this chapter, I would pull these out. Hopefully through that work you have uncovered a few things that you either want to try or you know without a shadow of a doubt fuel your soul. You also should have a good inventory of the pieces that could get in the way and can start working towards the changes needed in order to start practicing soul care.

Remember, getting to a starting place can be as involved or not as you need it to. If you journaled your way through this book and created some type of list, use it. If you have done nothing and you want to see what application could look like, just jot down three things you are interested in.

Seriously, don't make it complicated. I recently had a conversation with a friend, and she was asking me questions about this project.

She said, "I've been inspired by your painting. It makes me want to try it for myself and see how it makes me feel. I've never done anything like that before." If that is you, just choose one thing. Hopefully the words in these pages have ignited a spark to try something new, revisit an old haunt, or just create some space for an activity that could feed your soul.

Wherever you are in this journey, this next step in this process is about creating space to actually do it, and in my opinion, this is where the fun really begins.

Scheduling

The level of structure you need will depend on your personality. The Rachel Hollises of the world will organize the heck out of it and love it, but for me, as soon as I start putting anything into a stringent system, I am just asking for boredom to waltz in. I use something called a "sporadic schedule." This means that I look over the course of the month and ask, where do I have possible windows? If I want to paint, is there an afternoon or evening where I can do this? If so, I plan it and try to stick to it.

But if you are a consistent scheduler, you will need to check your barometer. If the activities start feeling like an obligation, I recommend scheduling fewer sessions. If you aren't feeling anything, then schedule more. This goes for sporadic schedulers as well. I find that my frustration and discontent is a great indicator of whether I have scheduled enough time to nourish my soul. If you find that you are moving through your days with less joy and more frustration, then look for more windows and schedule them.

This happened to me recently. I was just coming off a busy holiday season, travel with the family back home, and a few days left of vacation before heading back to work. I have several practices in play for times when things are really hectic, and I can't fit in good quality nourishment. But I was in a funk. I wasn't sure if it was being tired from travel and Christmas, some personal stuff I was dealing with, or all of the above, but I was struggling to find joy in the moment, and it was really irritating me. I decided to take an afternoon when cleaning was needed and instead devote it to painting whatever I wanted to. It was just what I needed. I woke up the next day feeling refreshed and grateful. The rest of my vacation was sublime. It changed my whole attitude and perspective.

What's interesting was during this time, I was doing a good bit of checking out—social media, Netflix movies, and I even had time to rent a movie that I wanted to see—but I needed a little more structure in balancing these activities with something that truly nourished me. For me, it is sometimes less about scheduling and more about tuning into what I need in the moment, which requires a bit of self-awareness.

One thing that helps me is to use the "checking out *vs* feeding my soul" assessment to determine if I need to dial up or down. That's what is cool about this particular tool. It isn't a one and done type of thing. It doesn't take long, and it helps clue me into greater balance.

And here is the thing about balance: I don't believe that we are ever fully "in balance" because checking out is always easier than refueling. I promise, the more you do this assessment, the more you will know when something is off and you need to reassess. I think it's just healthy to recognize that when you are favoring only activities that allow you to check out, you must be sure to sprinkle in enough soul care to keep things healthy.

I also try to hold some weekends loosely. If you are a Type A, "I need everything planned" type of person, then you go for it. Plan the heck out of this. For me, I sometimes just need white space so I can feel the freedom to pursue something I love. This means in busy seasons I may opt to hold a weekend sacred by planning nothing "extra" into it. What this means is that if the kids have a soccer game or a recital, we don't plan other things that weekend. This also may mean that we skip church. I'm not saying this is for everyone, but when your world is in constant motion, not having anything extra planned can allow the extra time you need to do something for you, and maybe even with your family or that close friend you haven't seen in a while. Holding one weekend loosely a quarter or even a month can bring value to this process. I highly recommend it.

For a sample of what I try to do, please reference my calendar in the next activity. There are tools there for you to try this for yourself. And get excited. It's time to go play. It's time to nourish your soul. It's time to see what this whole thing is about. Hopefully you have some tools, and with this schedule, you are able to create the time (one of your biggest obstacles) to do it.

activity

Scheduling Activity

Nearly 90% of women I polled said the reason they don't create time for themselves is because they don't have the time. Circular reasoning, but I get it, because I'm in the same boat. I find the best thing to do is to physically get that time on your calendar. I usually use my Outlook calendar that has everything else on it, but I've provided these calendars as examples. I'm a sporadic scheduler. You will notice I just randomly choose times. Some of that is based on where I know I have more flexibility. Whatever your style, treating those activities you love like an appointment may just help you stick with them.

Example of my activities below:
- regular painting
- abstract painting session
- facial mask or bath
- book design
- beach vacation (yes, add that vacation- -it fuels my soul. It should be represented)
- family bike ride and nature walk
- parents here (enjoying loved ones feeds my soul. I'm capturing it)

List the activities you want to add to your calendar here:

_____

_____

_____

_____

_____

_____

_____

_____

_____

_____

_____

_____

Now, think through your schedule and what makes sense. In my example below, you will see that I don't have a lot of my creative practices the first two weeks of the month. This is because I have quite a few deadlines I'm working towards. You may also notice that I didn't schedule much for the last week. I will wait to fill in and assess what that week looks like and how I have fed my soul over the month. Based on those results, I'll schedule that week.

_____

_____

_____

_____

_____

_____

Here is an example of my calendar:

august

sunday	monday	tuesday	wednesday	thursday	friday	saturday
						1 beach vacation
2	3	4	5 bridge snack: face mask	6	7	8 book design
9	10 paint	11 bridge snack: bath	12 paint	13 parents here	14	15
16	17 paint	18	19 paint	20	21	22 afternoon paint session (focus: abstract)
23	24	25	26	27	28	29 family bike ride and nature walk
30	31					

I've provided a blank calendar for you on the next page. You can also find this blank calendar in my workbook (at a larger scale) by visiting www.alisonenglish.com/resources.

planning time to feed your soul

Blank Calendar

sunday	monday	tuesday	wednesday	thursday	friday	saturday

Feel free to fill in the month and dates above. You can either make this your "soul care" calendar or fill in with all the other things you have on your plate. Like I said, I use my Outlook calendar because it feels more like an appointment. Some of you may prefer to separate these things out. It is all up to you. The point is to schedule it and make it happen. Whatever makes you successful, do it.

16

"Bridge Snacks"

Once you start practicing your soul-nourishing activities, you may begin noticing that you start appreciating more things. You will come alive at random moments. You will begin to see the world through a brighter lens. Your gratitude will spark randomly, and you will begin seeing magic all around you. Again, I think this looks different for everyone, but in my experience, it unlocks an unleashing inside of me. It is beautiful.

But depending on your soul care activities and the time it takes to do them, you may not be able to get to them as often as you like. I mean, let's be real, if your go-to is a 4-hour hike on your favorite trail or running in races once a month, there is a good bit of space that exists between the times you get to do that thing you love.

This made me recognize that there are simple practices that I can put into the every day that seem to foster the same spirit of feeding my soul in between the times I can actually create. They are small, simple things that honestly surprised me. I call these bridge snacks.

A "bridge snack" is a term that I borrowed from dietician, Kelly

"bridge snacks"

LeVeque. She talks about them in her book *Body Love*. Kelly is a dietician to the stars, and I loved her approach. A bridge snack was a healthy snack that met certain criteria and helps your blood sugar not dip too far before you can get home to eat your healthy meal. It isn't chips or cookies or even fruit. It is a snack that is designed specifically to keep your blood sugar in check, steady and calm. It is satiating and makes your body feel good.

A metaphorical bridge snack does the same thing, and for me this looks like the warmth and glow of a candle, the sweet, warm taste of my coffee every morning, at least ten minutes of meditation every day, a walk along a beautiful path set to music, writing morning pages where I journal what is on my mind, a facial mask at night before bed, snapping pictures with my iPhone and sharing them with others, an occasional walk through an art gallery, daily sketches when I can't paint, striking a match when I light a candle.

To keep it easy to execute, I decided to make these things readily available. This allows me to do them when the notion strikes me. When I start to check out, I can ask myself, would I rather do a facial mask instead? I began prepping and keeping these things on hand, ready for when they would come to mind. I didn't schedule them— just made them a part of my routine, or if given the opportunity on a whim, I would take it. Knowing that they were ready helped me recognize the opportunity in the moment so I could foster this care for myself. They became bridges between the designated times I scheduled for feeding my soul, and I found that they helped allow the gratitude and the magic to linger a little longer.

I mentioned that these practices, made the new sense I discovered more acute. When I'm doing this well, I see little things. Magical moments happen more often. I wind up relishing the simple shadows dancing on the porch, the sun glistening through the trees, leaves falling gracefully as my kids ride their bikes under their boughs, or the drops of dew atop a tree branch as I walk out to my car in the morning. I see all these things, and it evokes a feeling of gratitude and awe that infuses my day. These things are there every single day, but in the hustle and bustle with everything on my mind, I don't see them. When I am giving my soul proper nourishment, however, they appear.

It's the combination of the scheduled times and the unscheduled practices that seems to produce the greatest results, and that's why I believe in learning to cultivate both. Again, this is not a stringent practice. I leave a lot of openness and grace. Usually it involves working in a moment, using spaces of time like taking a shower, getting ready for work, or even the wee hours of the morning to foster these feelings. Sometimes it is trading a Netflix show for a facial mask or sketching. Sometimes it is trading social media for candle lighting, meditation, and journaling. Sometimes it is just lighting a candle while I'm getting ready for the day or sitting out on my porch during the golden hour. All in all, they are fueling me—the little things and the big—and I feel the most in balance when they are being incorporated regularly.

activity

"Bridge Snack" Activity

Bridge snacks are those simple, easy ways that evoke a little joy or give your soul a little boost in between the times you are actually able to practice feeding your soul. These should be simple and easily accessible. I've given you a few examples below to get you started, but use the spaces below to create your own.

Once you have made your list, map them to an activity or day of the week when you might want to incorporate them. You can get as scheduled (or not) as you want. With just a little planning you can carry soul care into regular routines, which will help combat getting too depleted as you wait for your next opportunity to feed your soul.

Once you are done with this exercise, use the back of the card or make a separate list of the items you need to purchase. Once purchased, keep them in a place that is out in the open (it will remind you) that is easy to access.

A Few of My Bridge Snack Examples
Morning coffee--make this a part of my daily morning routine. Some mornings I'll sip on the front porch while I work on my morning pages.

Candle lighting with match--incorporate when I shower and dress, baths, and even when doing a facial mask. Add to regular activities like folding laundry or cleaning my room.

Facial mask--try to incorporate one night a week during my nightly routine.

Use the lines below to write your own list of "Bridge Snacks"

_____

_____

_____

_____

_____

_____

_____

_____

_____

_____

_____

_____

_____

17

The Importance of Human Connection

This topic came up over and over again in my interviews and in the surveys I did. I was trying to figure out how I would implement it in the book, and then a worldwide pandemic hit. As I write this, we are practicing social distancing. Restaurants are closed, and my kids are doing school virtually. I was pulled from a class and am now working remotely for at least the next 30 days, and the world has literally come to a stand-still. The craziest part about it is we can't come within 6 feet of another human being (unless we are in the same household). It's scary, nerve wracking, and difficult to even understand what to believe.

I'm sure we will learn a good bit through this very difficult time in our world's history, and I know without a shadow of a doubt that we will discover our need to slow down, enjoy our lives, and relish time with other people. It's not ironic that it takes something like this to help you truly appreciate many important and meaningful things in your life. It's human nature but there is nothing that breaks my heart more than to know that I can't even hug my friend in the grocery store should we run into each other. No in-person chats, no church, no work, no school, no parties, or meeting up for drinks, just complete isolation.

While I find myself on my front porch watching passers-by as we all try to get out of our homes but not interact with each other, it not only has me thinking about our need for human connection (we are wired for it), but the quality of it. What I have realized is that we can slice and dice human connection in a lot of ways. Some ways fuel us. A lot of ways don't. For example, when this topic came up with one of my single friends, Katy, she talked about how much it is a part of her need to care for her soul. Because she lives alone and is by herself much of the time, she truly needs quality interaction with close friends and family to feel nourished. In talking with her, I realized that I had come to take these interactions for granted. Not only that, I wasn't truly utilizing them to feed my soul.

It got me to thinking about my relationship with Katy. Every single time I get together with her, I feel energized and refreshed. She admitted the same thing. She and I, we are kindred spirits. We connected day one of our meeting, and we can go deep. We challenge each other and speak truth. We also love each other, too. Connection with her stirs my heart, and it feels like a breath of fresh air.

I have other interactions that are surface in nature. I think these play a role too. It might be fun, lighthearted, and you just walk away having a good time. I have lots of interactions like this, and I'd be sad if they went away.

But then there are those interactions with people by which I feel drained. I had a relationship once where every time I would walk away from my time with that person, I just felt like I had absorbed her negativity and complaining. I'm down for being there for people when they need it, but when your friendship looks like this for years, it probably isn't healthy!

Another type of connection that can drain me is the one where gossip is the center of the interaction. I have been known to get caught up in in the heat of a good gossip session. It's not something I am proud of, and when I walk away, it just doesn't feel great.

I share these examples because I think you can look at human connection through the lens of soul care. When connecting with others are you checking out (good fun interaction leaving you lighthearted and upbeat) or feeding your soul (those deep-seated conversations that stir your heart and make you feel encouraged)? How are you evaluating your relationships, and how are you showing up to them? Are they helping you or getting in the way?

In this season of uncertainty and after my conversation with Katy, I've realized that I'm not really doing a good job with either—not with my friendships and not with my family members. I'm going through a lot of motions, checking a lot of boxes, and I'm giving little time to fostering rich connections with the people I love and care about most.

If it helps, you may want to take an inventory of your current closest relationships and ask yourself the question, which of these relationships would I like to go deeper on, to approach more with a lens of soul care? How often should I be scheduling time with these folks, and what are some ideas I could discuss with them or implement in our relationship?

You may also want to ask yourself which of these relationships are draining you. Are they toxic? Do you need to create some space or even have a conversation on how you would like the relationship to change? I know these are hard conversations and should be evaluated with a lot of intention.

My intent here is not to stir up drama between you and your friend or loved one. My intent is to challenge you (and myself) to seek more interactions that fuel you, not drain you. You are the only one who can figure that out.

18

Too Much of a Good Thing

You have worked through understanding more about who you are and what you love and you possibly have discovered what feeds your soul. You're ready to combat the obstacles and excuses that lay before you and set out to create an intentional, regular practice of soul care. Now I'm going to caution you about one thing: you can always have too much of a good thing. It is no different than enjoying too much food over time. Just like overeating, you can find yourself crossing over into feeling overly full, sick, or even nauseous.

We need physical nourishment every single day, but overindulgence means potential sickness, weight gain, indigestion, and health problems. Not enough and we starve. And sometimes a good old fast helps enliven the gut, cleanses the system, and helps you savor your favorite foods when you taste them again.

I share this because some of you have the discipline of an Olympic gold medalist, and I envy you. Some of you get consumed by your passions and can start using soul care like a drug—looking for hit after hit. But remember, it is balance that you are seeking. Over time, when you are overindulging, you may discover that you start getting bored. You may find that the joy is gone. You may feel like it is becoming more of an obligation and that it doesn't work anymore.

This happened to me when I started painting; I couldn't get enough of it. I went to it over and over again. It was like I was on fire with ideas, playing with color, and learning techniques; and then I got into a rut. I started running out of ideas. I started getting bored with the same techniques. I started using it to feel approval. My ego got in the way. I tried a few things, and they only frustrated me, so I quit; and I quit for a really long time.

If one or more of your activities isn't bringing you joy, then it may be time to set up another date day or take a month off. What I find with overindulgence is that I generally start taking something for granted. It loses its luster. Sometimes I feel stumped or as if I'm painting or drawing the same thing, writing the same narrative, or walking by the same scenery. And it becomes routine and boring. These are signs it is time to switch it up, take a break, or seek out other inspiration.

It never fails. When I come back to a creative practice that fuels my soul, I am always reminded of why and how much I love doing that thing. But you can also take breaks for too long. I believe when this happened with painting, I stayed out of it for too long. I started letting a lot of excuses and obstacles get in my way, and I hadn't quite figured out the cadence for staying in balance. But when I came back to it, there it was. It was like a balm to my soul. I needed the break to appreciate the magic because I lost it in my overindulgence of it.

You don't have to nourish your soul all the time for it to work. It is

too much of a good thing

like any type of thing—too much of a good thing is no longer a good thing, and taking a break helps to tip the balance back into place.

activity

When to take a break assessment

This assessment is designed to help you determine when you may need to take a break from an activity that is feeding your soul. You can always have too much of a good thing, and if you answer "yes" more often than "no" to these questions, try taking a few weeks off to try something new.

Before your activity

Before you start your activity, ask yourself, do you feel a sense of dread and even a desire to put off your soul care practice? Are you not feeling excited about starting it, or do you feel a sense of indifference about it? Is your usual desire not there?

Answer below:

_____

_____

_____

_____

_____

_____

_____

_____

_____

_____

During your activity

While in the midst of your activity, do you feel yourself getting restless, bored, or even frustrated? Check in with your feelings and ask yourself, is this showing up during your favorite activity most of the time?

Answer below:

_____

_____

_____

_____

_____

_____

_____

_____

_____

_____

After your activity

After you have left your activity, do you feel frustrated? Is the joy gone? Are you feeling drained from it instead of energized? We all have off days, but if this happens more often than not, this may be an indication that you need to take a break.

Answer below:

_____

_____

_____

_____

too much of a good thing

_____

_____

_____

_____

_____

_____

_____

Remember this doesn't mean that you need to quit something. It just means you may need to take a break from it. The length of time you need is really up to you, but I find for me, sometimes it is just waiting until the itch or stirring returns. When I feel it, I get back to the activity. Only you can know, but hopefully this exercise can help.

You can find this worksheet, along with all the others, in the workbook available on my website at www.alisonenglish.com/resources.

"I would become the worst version of myself. Every day I would become less and less of the person that the people I love would want to be around."

Sarah Beth

Interlude

Sarah Beth's Story

I met Sarah Beth through a friend. She was single when I first met her. She is one of those beautiful souls that you meet, and you just feel drawn to.

Sarah Beth is a writer, and I've enjoyed reading many of her thoughts as they have been published on a variety of blogs. She also is in the gym a lot. Even during her pregnancy with her first child, she was there regularly.

I really tried to come to my interviews with few or no preconceived notions about the person, but I came to hers feeling like I knew what Sarah Beth would say. It just goes to show that we don't always know things about friends, and our perceptions are not always the reality.

I expected Sarah Beth to talk about her writing as a way she feeds her soul, but it didn't even come up. Instead, two topics emerged: the three things that she feels really fuel her and the shifts of these practices in a new life season.

She mentioned exercise and her Bible Study in the morning, which didn't surprise me given what I knew about her, but the activity that surprised me was cleaning. I do not receive any joy out of cleaning (other than the fact that I like things tidy *vs* cluttered and dirty), so it was hard for me to imagine. I was also surprised because I was expecting her to talk about writing, but what I love about this exercise is what fuels our souls can look different from person to person.

When I asked Sarah Beth what it was about cleaning, there were a few things that it brings for her. She had a theme that emerged in just about everything that brought her renewal and joy: solitude. Sarah Beth needs time with her thoughts, to process, to think, and to ponder. Cleaning is a place of solitude for her. It allows her to think and be quiet. "When things are clean, I process my thoughts, and I can breathe. It doesn't distract me," she said. "It also allows me to 'clean out' my own thoughts, which I desperately need."

"I over-analyze things," Sarah Beth confessed. As she cleans, it is not only allowing her to clean surfaces and spaces, but she is doing that mentally as well. "I think a lot about my future when I clean. It allows me to process my actions or thoughts, and by the time I'm done, I feel lighter all over." Interestingly, cleaning for Sarah Beth is not just about getting a job done; it is a therapeutic way for her to process and clear her mind. In those moments, she finds freedom and feels lighter and refreshed.

I asked her, if you didn't have these practices in your life, what would happen? Her response, "I would become the worst version of myself. Every day I would become less and less of the person that the people I love would want to be around." She even said, "Others that are not as close to me may not even notice, but my loved ones would definitely know and understand that I was not myself."

That's powerful, isn't it? The ones we love and who know us the best, the same ones we use to make excuses around why we can't care for ourselves in a way that nourishes our souls—they are the ones who feel the best and worst of us based on the state of mind we are in. It's a bit of a paradox.

But what was interesting about my conversation with Sarah Beth was this theme that emerged about seasons. I mentioned in the beginning that when I first met her, she was single; she then met her hubby, and she was only a few months into becoming a mother for the first time when I interviewed her for the book. Like many of us, when that first baby comes along, it's beautiful, wonderful, and hard.

I remember my mother telling me when I had my first child that time would shift for me. I asked how, and she said, "You will lose the blocks of time—the hours—that you once had. It will be an adjustment. They will one day come back, but there will be a season when blocks of time no longer exist, and it can be hard because in a sense you lose a bit of your freedom."

As soon as Sarah Beth started talking about her new season, I knew this was exactly what she meant. She used to spend a good amount of time journaling and reading in the morning before work. When I asked her about what that looked like now that the baby was here, she said, "My Bible study and quiet moments/reflection, they have come off the table. I could wake up earlier, but I'm just exhausted."

She expressed guilt over this, but I could tell she was also wrestling with just how realistic it was to expect this of herself. She referred to the new season—and we both agreed—new seasons require a bit of grace. Things don't necessarily have to go away. They may just look different.

She talked about her workout routine and said she's had to let a bit of that go as well. When a meeting goes long at work and she has 20 minutes instead of an hour in the gym, she takes the 20 minutes. At first this felt "wrong" for her health; but then taking the hour and not getting to her son by a certain time also felt wrong, and she decided to prioritize the time with her baby because now that she is back at work, those few hours after work are the few she gets with him.

Cleaning has had to change too. Starting a cleaning project doesn't always mean getting to finish it because the baby might need to feed, get upset, or need her attention, again cutting into the way she used to care for herself.

This was a huge aha for me. Life seasons impact a lot of things, and in talking with Sarah Beth, I realized a couple of things. She talked a lot about giving herself grace, which I think is absolutely necessary. You may fall into a period of resentment or frustration at your lack of freedom. You could feel the same way about having too much time (Kids are grown. Now you have more time on your hands and you don't feel as needed–I hear you, empty nesters). Your body, mind, and soul have been accustomed to getting a lot of attention, and now you are starting to feel depleted because you can barely figure out how to get dressed in the morning, much less out the door with your new baby. You have to transition into a new norm.

What I also realized in talking with Sarah Beth is that it is often in new seasons that we throw out a need for balanced self-care. In her case, she is just trying to survive most days and love on this little one that has totally rocked her world. She is full throttle into being a mother and doing it well. This is generally when (and I know because I did it) we throw out caring for ourselves and start suppressing our needs because we are in survival mode. This is all fine and good, but at some point you have to figure out your new norm. The hard thing is that by the time you come up for air, baby number two or three is on the way... and you are doing this all over again.

It's easy for seasonal changes to propel us into a place of feeling out of control. I asked Sarah Beth about this. How are you going to continue to care for yourself in the midst of all this change? She was still figuring it out. For her, it was looking for the little pockets of time and seizing them when they came, but she admitted she still wasn't sure; and a few months in with a baby, I think that is normal.

I want to challenge all of us not to allow a season to make us completely lose ourselves. Our seasons are not an excuse to fall off the wagon—they give us a creative opportunity to strive for balance. Give yourself grace and take an inventory. Periods of time doing things you love may be shorter or less frequent, or you may even drop an activity so you can make time for one that gives you more joy. It may be an opportunity for you to carve out a day date or a couple of hours to come up with some kind of plan forward—even if it is small. Don't allow your season to take control because it will. It always does.

I'm serious when I say you have more control than you think. Your new season just means you get to reset expectations, set boundaries, ask for help in a new way, and ask yourself hard questions again about what you want to spend those precious hours on. And one day, all too soon, you will be doing it again because the journey of life is all about seasons, and the purpose of feeding your soul is to help you enjoy every single one of them.

19

Practicing What I Preach

I am starting week ten of "sheltering in place" during the Covid19 worldwide pandemic. Ironic that it happened during the birthing of this book? I don't think so. It is interesting to me that this concept was birthed in my life, and then I was given the gift of the pandemic to test it.

Anyone who picks up this piece of work for the foreseeable future will know and understand what I am talking about. You will be able to recall where you were. You will be able to recall how you felt. You will be able to recall how drastically your life changed, how painful and hard it was. You will be able to talk about the blessings, the time, the learnings, and how it changed your life. Our experiences will be different, but the common denominator will be the same.

This season has been hard, and we aren't out of the woods yet. It's scary and difficult to navigate, and whether you are more fearful of the virus or the economic impact, the fact remains that nearly every sense of your being may be wrapped in distress.

The stress for me has been different from the stress I experienced at the start of this book. My soul was depleted, and I was burned out and tired. But the work was challenging, interesting, and hard, but in a very satisfying way. I felt stuck, but it was because I had failed to feed my soul. I lost myself in the process of doing work that I actually enjoyed.

The world around me was intact. I felt secure in my health, my surroundings, my finances, and my faith. I felt safe. That space of complete exhaustion—much of it was because I had failed miserably at creating healthy boundaries and caring for myself. I got carried away.

But this season is different. I feel trapped, not because I have put myself here, but because the world around me has changed. I can't get out. I have to stay away. Self-isolation is required. It's difficult to articulate, but since we have all lived through it, I feel like you know. Your feelings may be a bit different from mine, but there is a different level of mental and spiritual gymnastics in this season, and it effects every part of my person—my mind, my body, and my soul.

It's like the checkers game turned into chess; it's much harder and more complex, and the strategies to navigate are much different and somewhat more calculated. Again, people are not wired to be caged. We are wired for community, and I cannot describe to you the level of my intense yearning for time with people. To hug them. To sit with them. Never in my life have I realized just how much I took this piece of life for granted, and if this is one gift the pandemic has given me, I hope I never forget it for the rest of my life.

But this thing isn't over, and I knew early on that I would need to take on a "chess" strategy. I knew I would have to ride this wave with a lot of care. I decided to apply much of what I have learned about nourishing my soul to this season. The principles are really the same, but the stakes are very different.

It's hard to describe, but I haven't been myself. I know that I haven't. In the first few weeks, I realized that I had to watch what I put my mind to. Within a week I knew I had to turn off the news and limit how many articles I read online. Social media became a dark wormhole of our possible demise. It was unsettling and scary. I found myself drawn to the stories and yet completely unnerved by them. I knew things couldn't stay this way, and my goal was to figure out how to "do this" for the next four weeks (never dreaming that ten weeks later I'd still be living out social distancing).

I quickly knew that I had to tap into things that would bring me joy. We took walks every day. Spring erupted here in the South, and since being in nature is one way I feed my soul, it was easy for me to get fuel. I had hard days like everyone else, but I kept those walks, and I kept filling up my gratitude journal. But as the weeks turned into months, this became harder.

Here's the thing, there were no day dates to go figure this out, no travel for work to see new places. We cancelled our beach vacation, which feeds my soul to no end. There were no coffee dates or lunches with friends to talk through life. There was no experience of a great new place on date night with that fantastic craft cocktail or a dessert to die for.

Places became less inspiring as cities became ghost towns. There was little to no traffic, and every person maintained a distance of six feet, all while wearing a face mask. I couldn't sit on a park bench or lean on a railing to overlook a waterfall. We avoided hiking on the weekends to avoid crowds, and most of the things on my "day date" list for the year were off the table. I couldn't dine out. I couldn't walk through the zoo or go to the botanical gardens. Places where I found inspiration and soul care weren't an option.

This made me angry. It made me feel trapped. And I thought, how in the world am I going to stay sane through all of this, knowing what fuels me and so much of it unavailable? Well, I learned a few things, and I decided to apply some of the principles from my learnings about soul care. It was like my theory was being tested: did this really work in wild circumstances? Not only did I test it, but this season reaffirmed and even broadened my understanding. Here are some of the things I learned:

I didn't allow limitations to keep me from pursuing this ideal.

What is interesting about constraint is that it forces you to get innovative. The "lack of" actually helped me refine more of what fuels my soul. I was able to see many things that were nourishing me—even things I hadn't seen before. It helped me see the things in my life that still served this purpose, and it opened up areas that I needed to take a hard look at. I realized I was really taking relationships for granted. I wasn't being intentional with my children. It helped me understand how even a date night with my hubby was feeding my soul and how much I appreciated the experience because food tastes better in a beautifully designed space with attentive service *vs* take out-on my kitchen table.

I found new ways to feed my soul.

I learned that new things were fueling me; these things had been in my life, but either I took them too much for granted or I wasn't present enough with them to realize how they were serving me.

- One example is game night with my family. I'm not a gaming person. I never have been. If things get too competitive, I'm done.

We had participated in family game night plenty of times. I always enjoyed it, but there was something different about us all being together, spending hours over cards and laughing our heads off. The interaction filled me up, recharged me, and brought joy to my soul.

-        On our daily walks, I would generally find that one of my kids would walk alongside me and talk to me the whole way to and from our destination. The other would walk with my husband. I noticed how little I listened—just letting them talk, but not really paying attention, I started being more intentional, and this resulted in us pressing flowers, talking about plant life, vacations, friends, and even a baking cook-off between the kids. I realized that the talks—when I listened—gave me joy. Getting to know my kids in a more dynamic way was such a gift, and I was fascinated by their curiosity and interest in much of life that I had failed to appreciate earlier.

-        I found life in writing. I started blogging again. This is something I had let go of. I just didn't have the time, and I felt pressure to create a content strategy and apply my professional learnings to it. I let that all go. I started just writing about things I wanted to. I shared about our home buying experience and picking out paint colors. I shared about projects and things I was struggling with, and it became something that some days I absolutely needed to move through my feelings and find joy once again. Some posts I published and others I didn't, but it was the exercise of writing that fueled my soul, and it helped that I didn't put parameters around it.

-        Because I had more time, I allowed myself to enjoy that time. On a whim, I would decide to sit outside on my porch and just listen to music. I did the same on a run one afternoon. Close to a favorite haunt, I stopped exercising and decided to walk through a rose garden that I knew was open and nearby. I was all alone, surrounded by magnificent blooms. The air was cool, the breeze fresh, and the energy magical. Learning to listen to myself when I needed that space meant stopping in the middle of what I was doing and taking that moment to soak it all in. But it was in those still, spontaneous moments that I found nourishment. I started listening to myself and my needs in the moment and acting on them. In the past, I would have pushed them down, always convincing myself that I didn't have the extra 15 to 20 minutes to enjoy that moment. It's something I plan to continue doing going forward.

I showed up consistently to practices that I knew fueled me.

I decided during this pandemic that I would try to paint as much as I could throughout the week. I stopped scheduling it and started making it part of my routine after work. I'm still unsure if I will continue this practice once life resumes some normalcy, but it worked in this season because I was home. I discovered a new love for watercolor. I learned I love to paint flowers. I was able to master mixing colors, define strokes, and create a bit of my own style.

I think I have resisted making it a routine in the past because I didn't want to lose what makes painting magical for me. I wanted it to feel special. But in this season, I knew I would need something to get me through, and I was willing to risk it. Some days were more beautiful than others, but I felt nourished. It could be for 30 minutes or three hours. I kept coming back time and again, and it has given me so much in a season that has felt foreign and stressful.

I got curious again.

This time I focused less on activity and more on what was really going on inside. If there is anything I have learned through various and painful circumstances, it is that I tend to avoid what I am feeling. This time around was strange. It was something that I hadn't experienced before. No one had experienced it before. The entire world was trying to figure out how to move through this new normal in our lives. I started to intentionally journal about what was going on deep inside.

One of my daily practices is morning pages, which comes from Julia Cameron's book *The Artist's Way*. During this time, many of my morning routines took a bit of a hit, and there were days where I just didn't want to practice meditation, reading, or my morning pages. But my morning writing was the most consistent, and I needed it to process the feelings as they cropped up. This whole experience is like a roller coaster with one day being great and the next being really hard. Also, articulating my feelings of frustration, being at home all the time, and not seeing others was difficult to understand. I got curious. I processed through morning pages or came back to my journal later as things would hit me.

I'd say there has been a good bit of self-discovery during this season, and while journaling didn't always make me come alive, I did find that it was one of the ways to help me not feel bogged down. It became part of my "recipe" for feeding my soul, which brings me to my fifth learning.

I explored getting quiet and creating space with music.

I now had margin in my days. It was a strange sensation—to have time on my hands that I wasn't always sure what to do with. I had always prioritized getting quiet and creating space (once I understood it was a part of my soul care recipe), but formerly I did this when I was alone. In this season, I was never alone. The kids are home, the hubs is home, and it is never fully quiet. I had to learn how to quiet my soul and create space in a different way when sound and interruption were assumed. Ironically, I found this quiet through music. It's almost as if my ear pods became the vehicle for my escape.

"Music gives a soul to the universe, wings to the mind, flight to the imagination and life to everything"

Plato

I talk about a soul care recipe in this book, but I never really talk about music, even though I have known for a long time that it brings me alive. I've been too distracted to see how music plays a significant role in not only preparing me for nourishing my soul but even in the activities of my soul care. Generally, music is playing when I'm meditating. Music brings my creative practices like painting alive. Music brings me into worship with my God, and music motivates and inspires when I'm out in nature. Music brings joy and gratitude in quiet spaces. I've now added listening to music to my own personal soul care recipe because in this season I realized just how much life it was giving me.

I realized it is okay to mourn.

I come to my soul care activities to find gratitude, joy, and life. That is generally what they bring, but I also found that there were moments during this difficult time when I was flat out sad while doing something that I loved. I found this perplexing. Was feeding my soul not serving me? Was I doing something wrong? Wasn't nourishing my soul supposed to always make me feel better? And then I realized, soul care is not a drug. It is not there to placate me or make me feel numb. It is not there to give me a high, so I don't have to think about or feel the things that are hard in my life. Nourishing my soul is there so that I can feel. I can identify. I can see.

You see, in this season, finding ways to nourish my soul allowed me to process my grief graciously. It allowed me to feel the pain more softly—to work through my feelings, own them, and acknowledge them.

One afternoon when I was out for a run, I was struck with my grief over this entire situation. I realized I was pushing back the feelings I needed to process. I was running along in one of my favorite parks. The weather bright, breeze light, spring still in bloom. Tunes were playing in the background as I rounded a corner and stopped. I stopped dead in my tracks as grief washed over me. It was like I couldn't hold it any longer. I wanted to cry, but I couldn't. I wanted tears to wash over my face, but I could feel myself resisting. I had known the pain was there, and I had been avoiding it.

And in that moment, I decided to stop, pause my run, and take a quiet moment. I walked over to some steps and took a seat. I watched as couples walked together, runners passed by, and a group of friends sat around (socially distancing), and I mourned. I let myself feel my sorrow, my frustration, and my sadness.

I sat in nature with my music turned up, and I allowed myself to feel the breeze wash over me. I have no idea how long I sat there— maybe through three or four songs. I kept telling myself that it was okay to mourn. It was okay to feel sad, and then I just got quiet.

The wind picked up. Large trees lined the pathway that was out in front of me, and as I sat underneath the boughs of those trees, the leaves started rustling in a gentle, beautiful dance. It was almost like the trees were waving at me, and in that moment, I felt God's presence.

He had felt distant. I know I'd been angry. He's all powerful, right? Then why did He allow this to happen? I still don't know, but in that moment, I felt Him there; and as the trees continued to wave at me softly, the sunlight casting shadows on the ground, I was moved at the simple beauty that I experienced in that moment. I've shared before that in these moments I have recognized them as gifts from above. I knew that moment was a gift from God to me. He was saying, "I'm here. I created this moment under the trees just for you. It's a gift just to say, 'I love you,' and it will be okay."

In the utter depths of my being, this is really what happens more times than not when I am nourishing my soul. It is this beautiful, spiritual moment that fills me up and either creates gratitude or soothes the weariness and sadness I am experiencing.

Never look at soul care as a drug, or an idol, or a way to escape your pain. Look at it as a way to work through your feelings and find gratitude and comfort on the other side.

In Conclusion

I remember the first time my father took me to a gourmet restaurant. It was a few months before I was married. I was twenty-three years old and my version of a nice place was a steakhouse you could find in any major city or that seafood chain that offers a lobster feast with a bib. Don't get me wrong, these places are good, but this was my first fine dining experience. This restaurant existed in one place with one executive chef, and their menus were based on serving what was fresh from the local area.

It was like my last hoorah with my dad before he gave me away. One-on-one dates with us had always been his thing. He wanted that last date to be special. He took me to a place on the Gulf coast where Presidents dined, and I will never forget the ambiance, the service, and the whole experience.

But to this day I cannot remember one single thing I ate except for the very first bite of my first course: a shrimp bisque. It was the most heavenly and delightful thing I had ever put in my mouth, and it still makes my mouth water. It spoke to me in a way that food had never spoken to me before, and it opened my eyes to the absolute joy and adventure that can be had through the creation of a gourmet meal.

That smooth texture, buttery taste. It was the perfect blend of seasoning and I savored every bight. Even eighteen years later, I can still taste it.

My friend, the potential for savoring this experience, this magic, this joy, exists in so many things; and my guess—if you are still reading this book—is that you may have needed the reminder, or like me with that meal with my dad, you need the discovery.

If you have never found the thing that opens your world to a heavenly experience, then I hope you will use this information I have shared here as your invitation to go explore, to try, to say no to things, and the invitation to sit at your own table and allow yourself that joy and beauty that will come by enjoying what feeds your soul.

As I mentioned in the quote I used at the start of this book:

"One life on this earth is all we get, whether it is enough or not enough, and the obvious conclusion would seem to be that at the very least we are fools if we do not live it as fully and bravely and beautifully as we can."

Fredrick Buechner

I truly believe that living fully and bravely and beautifully will be hard without this intention. For me, living out and practicing feeding my soul—nourishing it, cultivating, and prioritizing it—is a primary piece of living a full, meaningful, and beautiful life.

I hope you will join me at the table. Now, where's the feast?

Reference List

While these books are not on this topic, I used quotes or references from these works. I recommend all of them if their topics in any way interest you.

Daring Greatly by Brené Brown
Everything Belongs by Richard Rhor
The Artist's Way by Julia Cameron
Body Love by Kelly Leveque
Big Magic by Elizabeth Gilbert
Boundaries by Henry Cloud and John Townsend

Some of the articles used to research the origins of Soul Food:
https://www.blackfoodie.co/the-humble-history-of-soul-food
http://www.oprah.com/food/the-origin-of-soul-food-african-american-cooking_1/all
https://firstwefeast.com/eat/2015/08/an-illustrated-history-of-soul-food

Acknowledgements

Thank you to my talented and much more eloquent sister, Emily, for being the first to read my first draft. Thank you for your honesty, counsel, and encouragement to keep going.

Thank you to my friends, Amber and Rachel, for talking through the concept with me and cheering me on to the finish line.

Thank you to my friend, Charlotte, for giving me perspective from another view and another angle around the whole metaphor. You continue to teach me so much!

To Rebecca, Elizabeth, Charnelle, Brittany, Laura, Sarah Beth, and Katy, thank you for being willing to interview and allowing me to share pieces of your stories here.

Thank you to my editors, Gina and Claudia. Gina, thank you for helping me piece this first book together and finding all the things I seemed to say too many times. Claudia, thanks for making my writing stronger by meticulously editing my words.

Thank you to my children, Charlotte and Douglass, for allowing me to work on this book when I'm sure you would have much rather that I attended to your needs. You are my world!

Thank you to my parents for cheering me on when I wanted to doubt myself.

And thank you to my husband, Doug, who throughout the process honored the space that I needed all while encouraging me not to sell myself short. Thanks for always being my biggest advocate and cheerleader. I love you!

About the Author

Alison English is a creative, dabbling in watercolor, abstract art, photography, and surface pattern design. She is now adding author to that ever-growing list in the publishing of this book. When she isn't writing books, painting or working her day job, you can find her and her family fixing up their 100-year old bungalow or exploring all the wonderful eateries in her area.

Alison resides with her husband, Doug, and their two children, Charlotte and Douglass, in Atlanta, Georgia. You can find her works available on her website at www.alisonenglish.com.

Made in the USA
Columbia, SC
20 July 2021